CW00503194

BRITAIN'S HERITAGE

1960s Childhood

Janet and John Shepherd

AMBERLEY

Acknowledgements

The authors would like to thank the following for their kind assistance in the completion of this book: Pat Carter, Graham Carter, Brenda Corn, Melinda Cutting, Mark Dunton at the National Archives, Luci Gosling at the Mary Evans Picture Library, Margaret Heppell, Sally Jones, Simon Jones, Sandra Lee, Stephen Lee, Karen Livingstone, Keith Livingstone, Vivien Mathieson, Geoff Shepherd, Heather Shepherd, Ann Stephens, Colin Stephens, Debra Wade, Stephen Wade.

Finally, a very special word of thanks to Les Waters and Rose Waters for their expert technical advice, good humour and patience, and to our commissioning editor, Nick Wright, for invaluable help and support. Any remaining errors and omissions are entirely the authors' responsibility.

About the Authors

Dr Janet Shepherd gained her doctorate in Poor Law Education at London Guildhall University. She is co-author with John Shepherd of *1920s Britain* (2010), *1970s Britain* (2012) and *1950s Childhood* (2014) for Shire Books and *The 1950s Home* (2017) for Amberley Publishing.

Professor John Shepherd has worked at the University of Huddersfield since 2010, and was previously joint director of the Labour History Research Unit at Anglia Ruskin University. His many publications include *Crisis? What Crisis: The Callaghan Government and the British Winter of Discontent* (MUP, 2013).

First published 2018

Amberley Publishing
The Hill, Stroud
Gloucestershire, GL5 4EP

www.amberley-books.com

ISBN 978 1 4456 8320 1 (paperback)
ISBN 978 1 4456 8321 8 (ebook)

British Library Cataloguing in Publication Data.
A catalogue record for this book is available from the British Library.

Printed in the UK.

Contents

1

Introduction

Family life for most children in 1960s Britain was very different from the previous decade. Full employment began to boost spending and brought relative affluence for many households as a new word, 'consumerism', appeared in the English language. More children grew up in comfortable homes, with indoor sanitation, television and disposable cash for luxuries, modern electrical goods – and toys. For many families, but not all, it was a bright and hopeful time.

As increasing numbers of women entered the workplace, mostly working part-time, there were many homes with both parents in paid employment. The traditional extended family where parents could rely on nearby relatives to help with child care declined as, with the growth of the car and improvements in transport facilities, families became more dispersed.

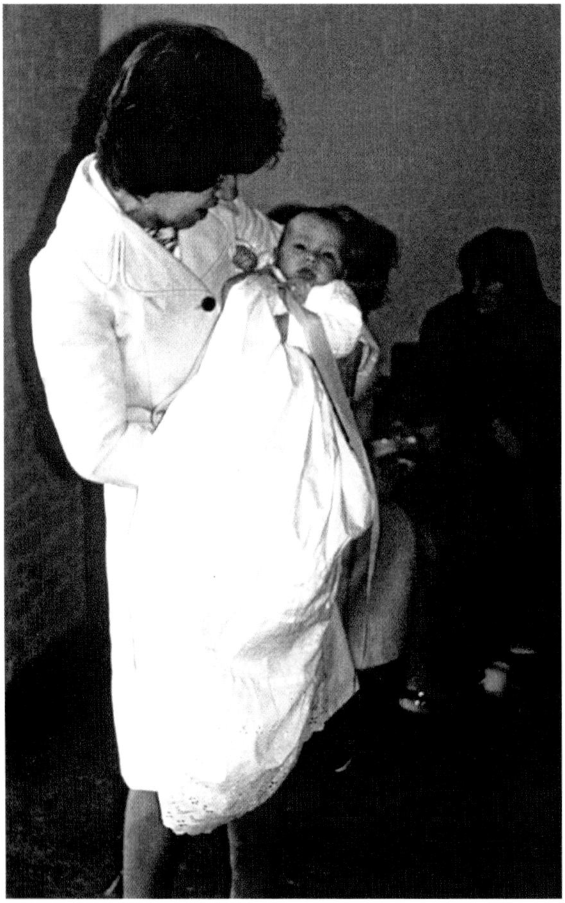

Nick Foster, christened in Cambridge, 1960, wearing a traditional long christening gown with a blue sash to indicate gender. Blue for a boy, pink for a girl was a 'rule' rarely broken. (Sandra Lee)

Did you know?

The bitter winter in 1962/3 caused huge disruptions to the sporting calendar. Some FA cup ties were rescheduled more than ten times and the football season was extended by four weeks.

It was the rapid increase in car ownership that most transformed family life. Labour MP Tony Crosland spoke for many when he said, 'All of us want the car and the greater feeling of mobility it brings.' School children visited massive car assembly plants, like Ford at Dagenham, and travelled in a Mini, the small car that spanned the decade. 'An icon of 1960s British popular culture', the Mini appeared in 1959 and was marketed for the whole of the next decade. In September 1964, in its first issue, *The Sun* emphasised how life had changed: '... cars, houses, refrigerators, washing machines, are no longer the prerogative of the "upper crust" but the right of all.'

At home, television heralded a new era. Children and adults watched more and more programmes, most notably game and variety shows and sport. With only three channels – BBC 1, ITV and BBC 2 – and usually just one television set, families frequently watched the same programmes together. England's phenomenal success in winning the 1966 Football World Cup was viewed by millions of people of all ages.

In education, there were important changes across all the sectors. By the late sixties, teaching and learning in primary schools became more child-centred. The rapid growth of comprehensive secondary education across Britain from 1965 gave rise to polarised debates. In higher education, far more places were available with the creation of a tranche of new universities.

The evolving National Health Service (NHS) saw marked advances in family health care, with the arrival of the contraceptive pill and new vaccines to combat some crippling childhood diseases. The liberalisation of society had a critical bearing on family life. Abortion

Two families enjoying days out with the car. An Austin A40 at Heacham Caravan Park and touring the Lake District by car in 1968 – with an original metal AA badge on the car. (Pat Carter and Margaret Heppell)

Family portrait. Sally and Stephen Martin, expertly photographed at home by their mother. Sally had two spotted dresses for primary school, one red, one blue, with matching bows. (Sally Jones)

was legalised in 1967, freeing many women from the fear of unwanted pregnancies. Divorce laws were relaxed, easing some of the stress for both parents and children, and by the close of the decade suicide was decriminalised and capital punishment had been banned.

Among the younger generation a cultural revolution was underway. British teenagers were at the heart of a new, vibrant youth culture. Modern popular – 'pop' – music saw the emergence of iconic bands like The Rolling Stones and, above all, the Beatles. Young people began to dress differently from their parents and adopted colourful modern styles, famously epitomised by the miniskirt. Terms like 'Swinging Sixties' and 'Permissive Era' were heard, linked by some to the sexual freedom associated with the arrival of 'the pill'. Teenagers voiced concern for global problems; in 1960, schoolboys at Highbury School in North London raised £1,000 for World Refugee Year.

In 1960, the relaxation of censorship laws meant an unexpurgated version of *Lady Chatterley's Lover* could legally be published. In 1963, Bob Dylan sang 'The Times They Are a-Changin' and poet Philip Larkin, born in Coventry and working at Hull University, reflected in 'Annus Mirabilis' on the dawn of a different social order:

> So life was never better than,
> In nineteen sixty three, (Though just too late for me),
> Between the end of the "Chatterley" ban,
> And the Beatles' first LP

The 1960s brought rapid technological and scientific innovations. London's impressive Post Office telecommunications tower in 1966 became a permanent symbol of the decade's progress. For children, science, technology and 'the space race' soon began to be reflected in the toy industry.

Despite growing prosperity, there was an increasing North/South divide. Surveys revealed that across parts of the Midlands and North, many inner city and rural children still lived in poor homes with outside toilets and inadequate heating. Increasing numbers of high rise blocks led to new concerns about social and safety issues.

Right: An image of the first badge issued by the long running and highly successful children's BBC TV programme *Blue Peter*, in 1963. In 2018, a limited edition 'diamond' encrusted badge was released to celebrate the programme's fiftieth anniversary.
Below: Two sets of stamps issued in 1969 to celebrate the new Post Office Tower and advances in telecommunications and technology across the decade. (Stamp designs © Royal Mail Group Limited)

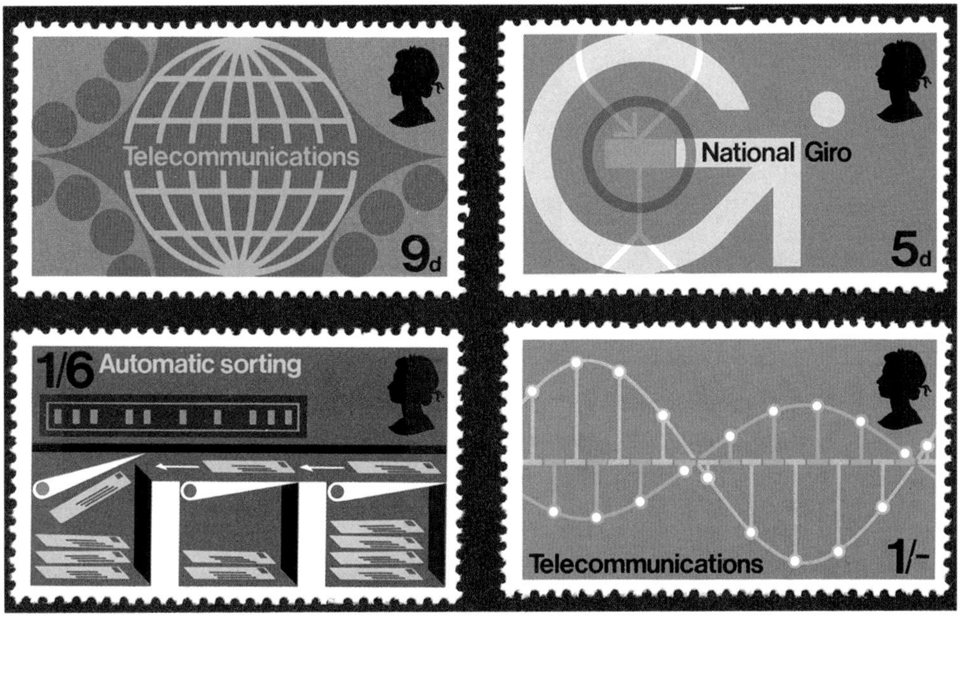

World events, particularly the assassinations of President Kennedy and Martin Luther King, had a huge impact in Britain. In July 1969, children and adults across the world watched television in amazement as US astronaut Neil Armstrong became the first man to walk on the moon. It was 'one small step for [a] man, one giant leap for mankind'. The young Stephen Wade marvelled: 'I still feel privileged to have witnessed mankind's greatest ever achievement.' It marked the close of a modern, controversial decade.

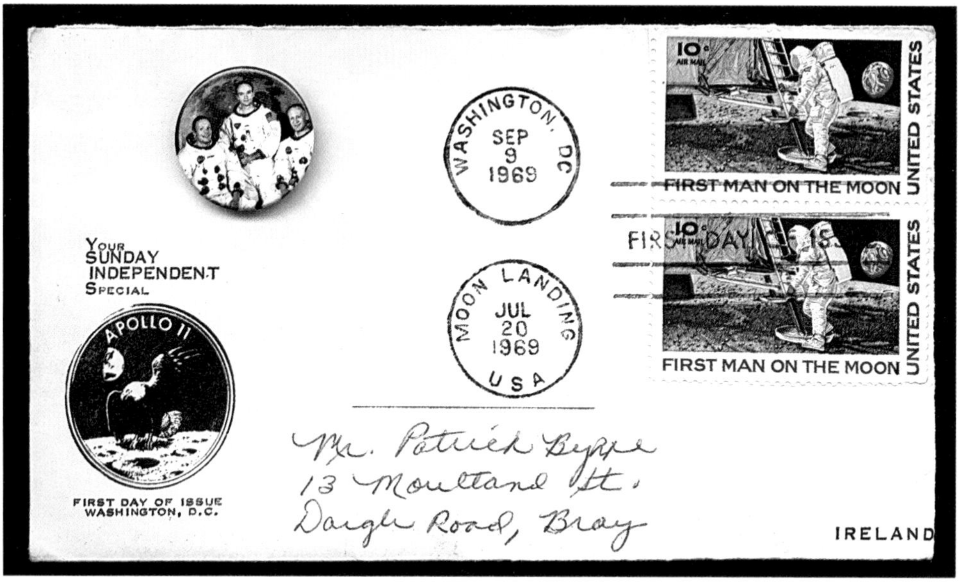

Above: Souvenirs from the USA's Apollo 11 moon landing on 20 July 1969. Six hours after landing, Neil Armstrong became the first human to walk on the lunar surface. Later, celebratory souvenirs became very sought after. (Janet Shepherd)

Left: Four young children enjoy playing in a small blow-up garden paddling pool on a warm June day in 1967. (Margaret Heppell)

2

Home Life

Many children raised in the 1960s enjoyed fundamental improvements in domestic life. New technology brought modern household goods, television and, above all, the arrival of the family car. However, while some children enjoyed comfortable housing, contemporary surveys revealed others endured shocking deprivations.

The major housing crisis, so dominant in the post-war years, continued. Slum clearance saw many inner city families rehoused into new towns. One of these was the town of Milton Keynes in Buckinghamshire, designated in 1967 and famously built on a modern grid road system. Others included Bracknell in Berkshire, Redditch in the Midlands and Livingston in Scotland. Families who remained in inner cities were increasingly moved into tower blocks on council estates. By 1969, there were around 400,000 high rise blocks across Britain. Although they were more comfortable

Baby congratulations card sent to celebrate the birth of a boy. Children were often still told that storks brought babies or even that they might be found under gooseberry bushes. (Sally Jones)

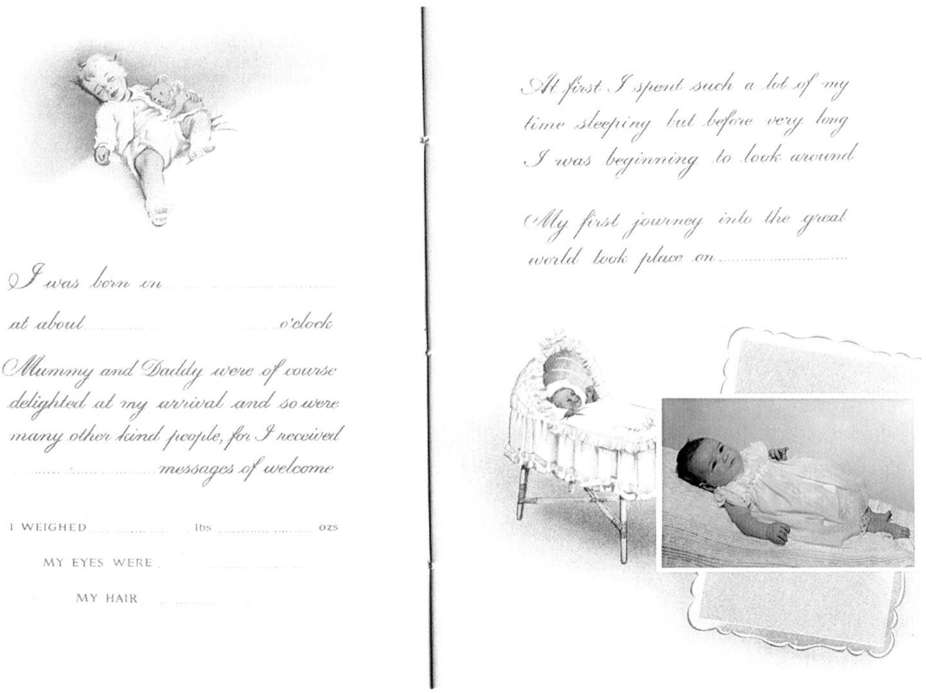

Debra Kirstie Livingstone, born October 1963. The modern spelling of 'Debra' instead of the more formal 'Deborah' became increasingly used. A baby book, this one produced by Nestlé, was used to record babies' achievements from birth to school age. (Debra Wade; the image is reproduced with the kind permission of Société des Produits Nestlé SA)

and sanitary than city slums, many new residents, especially young mothers with small children, felt isolated. The height of the blocks meant children could not easily be sent outside to play. Lifts were frequently not working and safety regulations compromised. Following a gas explosion, East London's twenty-two-storey Ronan Point partially collapsed in 1968, killing four people. Only two months old, the flats were found to have been poorly constructed. Fire ladders only reached half-way up the 200-foot high rise – a sad precursor of the 2017 Grenfell disaster.

Poor regard for safety led to a national tragedy when one of seven slag heaps above the Welsh village of Aberfan collapsed on 21 October 1966. The catastrophic coal slide engulfed Pantglas Junior School, killing 116 children and twenty-eight adults. The National Coal Board was blamed for ignoring safety regulations and allowing the slag heap to be situated over an underground spring of water.

By the mid-sixties, worrying facts about poverty emerged. A 1965 study, *Poor and the Poorest*, by sociologists Peter Townsend and Brian Abel Smith led to the establishment of the Child Poverty Action Group. Statistics revealed that half a million undernourished children were in homes where the father earned less than the benefit level. The Labour MP Alan Johnson was born into a very poor London family and remembers being constantly hungry: 'I've never forgotten that emptiness and craving for food.'

In 1966, film director Ken Loach's hard-hitting BBC television drama *Cathy Come Home* highlighted the true extent of poverty and homelessness. Televised at a popular viewing time,

Eight young boys pose cheekily for the photographer in a Sheffield city street, 1966. Children playing out in the street began to lessen as traffic increased but was still common in back roads, especially during the first half of the decade. (Mary Evans Picture Library)

it provoked a strong public outcry. Around the same time, the housing charity Shelter was formed by Des Wilson. Shelter focussed on inner cities, in Liverpool, Birmingham, Glasgow and London. By 1969, findings revealed 3 million people living in squalid, overcrowded, accommodation. Large families were often crammed into a couple of rented rooms. In Liverpool, 70 per cent of old houses were sub-standard. The city's Netherley Estate was later referred to in a Parliament as a 'tenants' nightmare'.

Immigrant families were among the very poorest. From former British Empire countries like India, Pakistan and Jamaica, immigrants were welcomed to relieve the British post-war labour shortage in the National Health Service (NHS) and the service industries. Between 1948, when the first group disembarked from the liner *Empire Windrush*, and 1970, nearly half a million people arrived from the West Indies. Tensions surrounding immigration reached a head in the 1958 Notting Hill riots and continued to fester. Many immigrants were already British citizens but were not welcomed. 'They used to say, go back home!' said Mandy, who arrived from the island of Dominica. The immigration 'issue' was brought home to millions by the racist character Alf Garnett in the sixties TV 'sit-com' *Till Death Us Do Part*. MP Enoch Powell's xenophobic 1968 'Rivers of Blood' speech warned of a coming apocalypse if immigration was not curbed. Although the 1965 Race Relations Act outlawed discrimination on the grounds of colour, race, or ethnicity, resentments continued and views became more polarised.

For most people, technology made a huge impact as the decade progressed. Washing machines, refrigerators and vacuum cleaners replaced hand washing, larders and carpet sweepers. Kitchens became brighter with colourful new plastics like Formica. Central heating and fitted carpets brought warmth and comfort and home telephones became more common. Modern plumbing transformed family life as indoor bathrooms replaced a tin bath in the kitchen. By the end of the decade, the number of homes without a bathroom dropped from 3.2 million to 1.5 million.

A 1960s kitchen, at the Willis Museum of Basingstoke Town and Country Life, includes a twin tub washing machine, Kenwood Chef mixer, vacuum cleaner and popular sixties crockery. A 1963 newspaper reports the assassination of President John Kennedy. (Willis Museum and Sainsbury Gallery: Hampshire Cultural Trust)

Did you know?

1960s designers were forward looking and progressive. Expendable items, like inflatable chairs and even paper furniture, appeared. In 1963, laminated, washable and colourful cardboard chairs, specially designed for children, were marketed as 'fibreboard furniture for the young'.

Shopping for food changed as small corner shops were replaced by supermarkets stocking a wider range of enticing products. After the austerity years, heavily sweetened cereals and 'instant' puddings like 'Angel Delight' had immediate child appeal. Manufacturers targeted children in their race for customers; for example, Brooke Bond put collectable and informative picture cards inside their packets of loose tea.

The increase in immigration brought more food from abroad. Numerous Indian restaurants opened, notably in London and the South East. The late 1960s saw the arrival of Indian and Chinese 'convenience' foods, like Vesta's Curries and Chow Mein. Italian influences introduced Spaghetti Bolognese and a variety of wines. Whether food came from home or abroad, there were no 'sell by' dates. Susan's father regularly washed the green mould off bacon before happily frying it in lard. Even with the growth of supermarkets, it was still quite usual for tradesmen to call. Milk was delivered daily and the post came up to three times a day. Many families paid in weekly instalments to obtain *The Children's Encyclopaedia Britannica* – with answers to almost everything.

Most children only received small amounts of pocket money. Woolworth's sweets counter attracted child customers with pennies to spend on new chocolate bars like Galaxy, Topic, and Toffee Crisp and sweet cigarettes, manufactured to look like the real cigarettes that many of their parents smoked. Despite a steady growth of ready-made shop clothes, many women still hand-knitted jumpers, hats, and gloves.

The major change in the home came with the growth of television. The TV, nicknamed the 'box in the corner' and frequently in colour after 1967, superseded the fireplace as the new focal point of the living room. Meals in front of the television replaced eating at a dining table and TV advertisements increasingly influenced food choices. In 1961, the 'Milky Bar Kid', a blond bespectacled young 'cowboy', made his debut promoting Nestlé white chocolate. It became one of the decade's best known advertisements. Many food stuffs, especially breakfast cereals, included tempting free gifts associated with popular TV programmes. Kellogg's Cornflakes and Sugar Smacks contained plastic badges and toys from children's science fiction television programmes, like *Captain Scarlet*.

Home knitting received a boost after the war when a greater range of colours and styles of yarn became available. Girls (not boys) were still taught knitting at school as a useful skill, not just as a hobby. (Sally Jones)

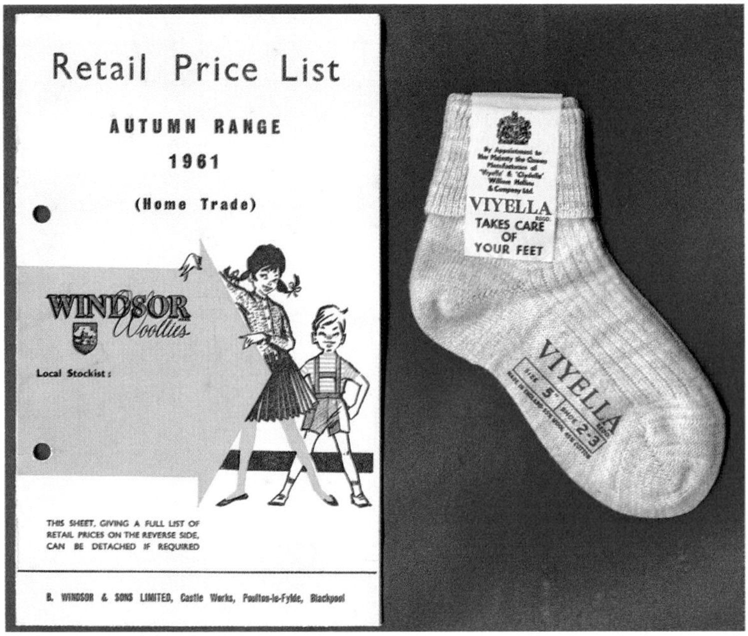

Windsor Woollies price list from 1961 and Viyella wool and cotton ankle socks: two quality children's clothing firms from the 1960s.

Did you know?

In 1964, BBC Radio's *Children's Hour*, aired on the Home Service (later Radio Four) between 5 and 6 p.m. every day of the week since 1922, came to an end. This followed a huge decline in readership brought about by the growth of television.

Children's television attracted a growing audience. Younger children watched *Play School, Camberwick Green* and *Trumpton*. Older children enjoyed the gameshow *Crackerjack!* and *Blue Peter* demonstrated things children could quite cheaply make at home. Mark Dunton made a model farm and loved *Blue Peter*'s famous catchphrase, 'Here's one I made earlier'. Whole families enjoyed shows like *Coronation Street* from 1960, *The Saint* and *The Avengers*. Popular game and variety shows included *Opportunity Knocks* and *Sunday Night at the London Palladium*, where one early presenter, Bruce Forsyth, soon became a household name. *The Morecambe and Wise Christmas Show* drew massive audiences across the decade. Watching football on television in the 1960s became almost universal. The first *Match of the Day* was broadcast in August 1964 on BBC 2, featuring a match between Arsenal and Liverpool. On Saturday afternoons at the Elephant and Castle, Stephen Wade recalled the local vicar knocking at the door in between conducting weddings, to check the score.

Interest in science, space and science fiction fuelled the meteoric rise of *Doctor Who*, first broadcast on BBC TV in November 1963. The introduction of the Daleks, extra-terrestrial alien machines, precipitated a rise in the ratings. By February 1964, the programme had over 10 million viewers. In 1968, Doctor Who's 'Swinging London' was invaded by Cybermen. Their bodies had metamorphosed from human flesh to plastic and metal – a nod to future

A colourful hand-knitted boy's jumper with a football design. The first completely non-leather football first appeared in the 1960s.

Many television sets in the 1960s were encased in rectangular wooden boxes. Modern thin-legged furniture became very popular after the dark, heavy furniture of earlier years. (Janet Shepherd)

Testament to the programme's huge success, the BBC advertised the Cybermen's third appearance on *Doctor Who* on the front cover of the *Radio Times* for the week 2–8 September 1967. (Radio Times)

prosthetic limbs. The series was famously described by the social activist Mary Whitehouse as 'teatime brutality for tots'. Mark recollected: 'I was part of the generation of boys and girls who watched *Doctor Who* with a mixture of fascination, excitement and terror, hiding behind cushions or the sofa.'

Despite the popularity of television, children still read books and comics. New books for young children included *Where The Wild Things Are* and *The Very Hungry Caterpillar*, while *Stig of the Dump* and *The Iron Man* appealed to junior ages. The first Roald Dahl books appeared – *James and The Giant Peach* and, in 1964, the internationally renowned *Charlie and the Chocolate Factory*. From the USA, Dr Seuss's classics like *Green Eggs and Ham* had universal appeal. Stephen learned to read from Rupert books and liked Marvel comics, especially *Spiderman* which his family collected from 'a dealer in the Old Kent Road'. Widely read girls' comics included *Judy*, and also *Bunty*, which unusually featured a working class heroine.

Cinema attendances declined after the arrival of television but musical films, especially from the USA, appealed to children. Favourites included *101 Dalmations*, *Mary Poppins*, *The Jungle Book* and *Oliver!*. The early James Bond films *Goldfinger* and *Thunderball* were watched by all ages; they broke box office records and suited the forward-looking sixties. *Whistle Down the Wind* in 1961, in which three Lancashire children think they have found Jesus hiding in a barn, saw the screen debut for a young Hayley Mills.

Car ownership doubled between 1960 and 1970 and revolutionised travel to work, day trips and holidays. Previously traffic free streets began to be filled with parked cars. There were no seat belts, or car seats for children, and as the number of cars grew, so did the accidents. Public information films warned of escalating traffic dangers. Road safety advertisements for children appeared on television, most notably the Tufty Club, which, by the close of the sixties, had over 2 million child members. The first pelican crossings appeared in 1969, with television advertisements explaining how to push the buttons to change the lights.

An adult reads to a very attentive four-year-old, Melinda Corn. The importance of parents reading to children was increasingly emphasised by primary schools during the sixties. (Melinda Cutting)

Italy's Fiat 500 was a practical and economical small car that was commonly seen on British roads in the late 1960s. (Janet Shepherd)

In popular books of the period, like those by Enid Blyton, children almost always played outside. Broadcaster Jeremy Vine helped his dad build a tree house in the garden that took three summers to complete. Children still regularly played in back streets, with bikes, roller skates, home-made go-carts, footballs and conkers. Collecting car number plates became a popular outdoor hobby, displacing the older pastime of collecting train numbers – the 'Beeching cuts' in 1963 led to the loss of 4,500 miles of track and over 2,000 stations.

It was not only the growing traffic that made playing outside seem more dangerous. The horrific 'Moors murders', when five children were killed by Ian Brady and Myra Hindley between 1963 and 1965, appalled the nation and brought a seismic change in attitudes to child safety. Afterwards, it was noticeable that fewer youngsters were allowed out and about without adult supervision. Organised groups, like Girl Guides, Boy Scouts or the Woodcraft Folk, provided safe opportunities to learn outdoor skills like orienteering, bird watching or how to light a fire but, as television attracted increasingly larger audiences, children spent less time in the open air.

The growth of car travel boosted trips to British seaside holiday camps. Donkey rides on the beach, metal buckets and spades, wooden deckchairs and 'Stop Me and Buy One' ice cream vans were all part of the enjoyment. Stephen regularly went to Sandown on the Isle of Wight to stay with his parents' friends but once journeyed to Scarborough, where 'our southern accents made us a centre of attention, as if visitors from another planet'. Travelling abroad for holidays provided new horizons for those who could afford it. In 1964, *The Sun*

Three colourful paper scrap pictures, popular for children to glue into scrapbooks, show children helping at home – walking the dog, watering plants and pruning a bush.

Tricycles were a very popular outdoor toy for younger girls and boys before they progressed to bicycles. Sally Martin and David Carter, both from Cambridge, enjoyed riding their 'trikes'. (Sally Jones and Pat Carter)

Girl Guide and Boy Scout groups continued to thrive in the 1960s, with their ethos of undertaking challenging activities, learning life skills and helping others. (Union Flag Scout Badge reproduced by kind permission of The Scout Association; Girl Guide Association)

A modern, heart-shaped children's paddling pool in Seaton, Devon, built in the 1960s. Girls usually wore one-piece swimming costumes rather than bikinis.

stated: "Five million Britons now holiday abroad every year...' This figure rose to 7 million by the late sixties as the growth of the package holiday industry meant foreign travel became less expensive.

Most children growing up in the 1960s benefitted from the upturn in the economy as more disposable cash brought a modern comfortable lifestyle. However, the decade also revealed the darker side of child poverty, leading to greater public awareness of growing social divisions between the 'haves' and 'have nots'.

Above left: Two postcards sent by a child holidaying in Blackpool to his grandmother in Willenhall, Staffordshire, in 1965. Blackpool was a very popular holiday resort for families in the north of England.

Above right: Children playing in the sand on the beach in front of a row of yellow chalets at a British holiday camp in the early 1960s. (Mary Evans Picture Library)

Below: Holidaying abroad. Debra and Karen Livingstone, aged six and four, enjoy a pony trek with their father in Cyprus in summer 1969. (Janet Shepherd)

3
Health

2018 marked the seventieth anniversary of the National Health Service. By the 1960s, babies, children and teenagers received progressively better medical attention than earlier generations. Public surveys revealed that most people supported the NHS. It was a key decade for seminal advances in birth control with the advent of the contraceptive pill in 1961. Until 1967, the new contraceptive could only be prescribed to married women, but between 1962 and the close of the decade the number taking 'the pill' rose from 50,000 to a million. Parents could determine the size of their families and by the end of the decade more children were being raised in smaller family units.

A 1960s *Family Doctor* magazine included a special 'Doctor's Orders' booklet, published by the British Medical Association (BMA), with advice on health and nutrition for parents of young children. (Reproduced by kind permission, British Medical Association)

Did you know?

On 30 October 1960, the first kidney transplant in Britain was performed on an identical pair of twins at Edinburgh Royal Infirmary Hospital. The procedure was a success, with both donor and recipient living for a further six years before dying from an unrelated cause.

The start of kidney transplants and the increasing use of Cardiopulmonary Resuscitation (CPR) saved many lives. Hip replacements were a major advance and the decade ended with the first UK heart transplant in 1968. By 1969, 'genetic engineering', promising hope for many families, was on the horizon. There was growing public interest in all things medical, particularly in the cinema and on television. Popular films included the 'Doctor' comedies, which continued from 1960 to 1966 with *Doctor in Love, Doctor in Distress* and *Doctor in Clover*. Television dramas that secured huge audiences included ITV's *Emergency Ward 10* and the BBC's *Dr Finlay's Casebook*, based in the fictional Scottish town of Tannochbrae.

Before 1967, the fear of an unwanted pregnancy was very real. The horror of illegal abortions by back street abortionists hit television screens in 1965 with Ken Loach's play *Up the Junction*. 'Anyone who saw that drama ... knows the evil we are discussing,' declared Lord Stoneham in a Parliamentary debate. The 1967 Act made abortion legal up to twenty-eight weeks, if carried out by a registered physician. Calls to reform the abortion law had escalated after the thalidomide tragedy in the early 1960s. Thalidomide had been marketed as a

Large carriage-built prams were very popular in the sixties. Pedigree advertised a 'flat spring chassis to give the softest of rides'. Today, vintage Pedigree and Silver Cross prams are collectors' items.

Cow & Gate milk and cereals were advertised as 'The Food of Royal Babies', encouraging 'sturdy muscles, strong bones and a healthy constitution'.

mild sleeping drug, safe for pregnant women. Tragically, many expectant mothers who took the tranquiliser gave birth to children with deformed limbs. In 1968, some of the afflicted children were awarded damages against the marketing company, Distillers. It was the worst medical tragedy in the twentieth century.

By 1966, 70 per cent of all British babies were delivered in hospital, where the care of new mothers and young babies differed greatly from 2018. Mothers in NHS hospitals regularly remained for ten to twelve days, confined to beds and bedpans until at least day three. Fathers were banned from delivery rooms and were only permitted to visit maternity wards for short periods. Despite the natural benefits of breast-feeding, many babies were routinely bottle-fed and placed in a communal nursery at night. Washable towelling nappies were used because disposable nappies were unreliable and expensive.

At the start of the decade, hospital ward regimes were strictly enforced. Matrons and senior nursing staff wielded considerable authority. Young student nurses were routinely allocated menial tasks and, in some hospitals, were not allowed to speak to the Matron unless specifically addressed. Beds had to be made with 'hospital corners' to ensure a pristine appearance before the arrival of the doctors on their daily rounds. The 1966 Salmon Report on nursing gradually introduced management changes resulting in the end of the traditional hierarchical role of the hospital matron.

With the development of special baby care units and ground-breaking neonatal medical technology, the care of sick and premature babies in hospital improved considerably during the sixties. Facilities at the Queen Elizabeth Hospital for Children in Hackney included a flat where parents could stay while their children were being treated. The Royal Manchester Hospital for Children was one of the first to allow mothers to sleep in the same room as their sick babies. London's world-famous Great Ormond Street Hospital established the first childhood leukaemia research unit, the first heart and lung bypass machine and pioneered treatment for hydrocephalus. For older children in hospital, visits from parents were encouraged but restricted. When a young Alan Johnson had appendicitis, visiting was 'half an hour every weekday evening, an hour on Saturdays and not at all on Sundays'. For some disabled children, hospitals could become permanent homes. In the late 1960s, a disturbing report into one British hospital discovered an impersonal regime where staff rarely interacted or played with the children.

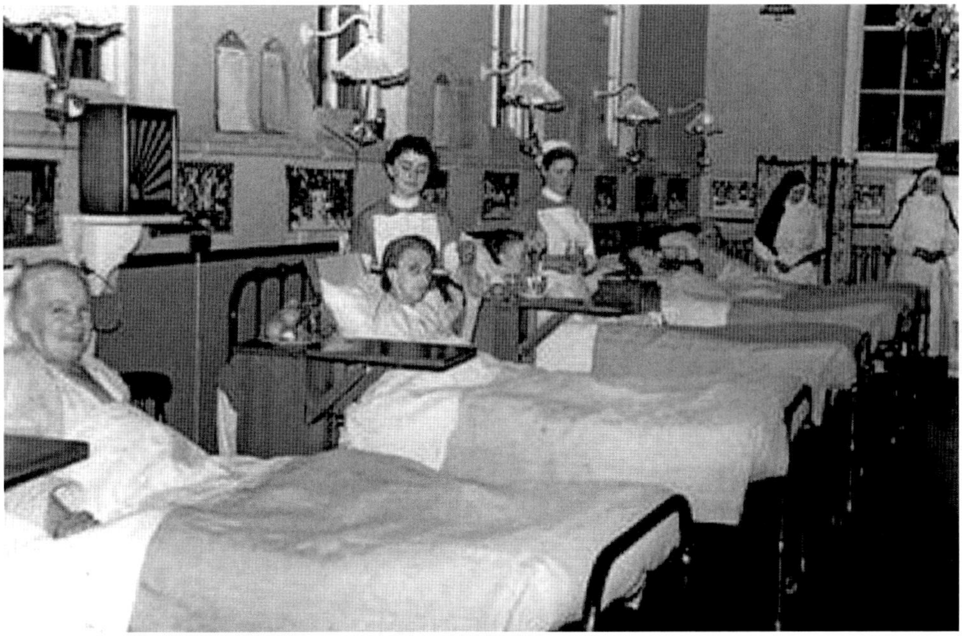

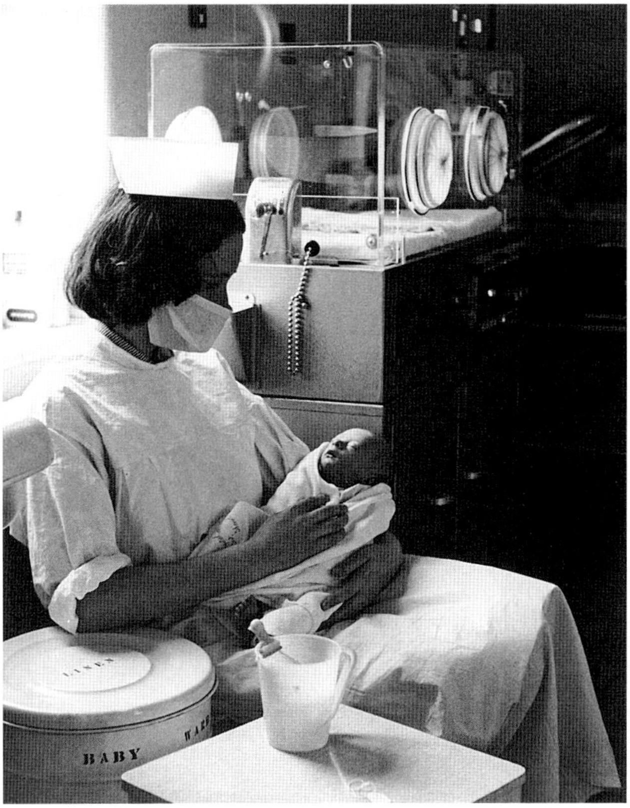

Above: A typical hospital ward in 1960. Student nurses undertook three-quarters of all hospital nursing under the supervision of ward sisters and a matron. (Janet Shepherd)
Right: A small baby being bottle-fed by a specialist nurse in a premature baby unit. Incubators were commonly used for sick and premature babies. (Mary Evans Picture Library)

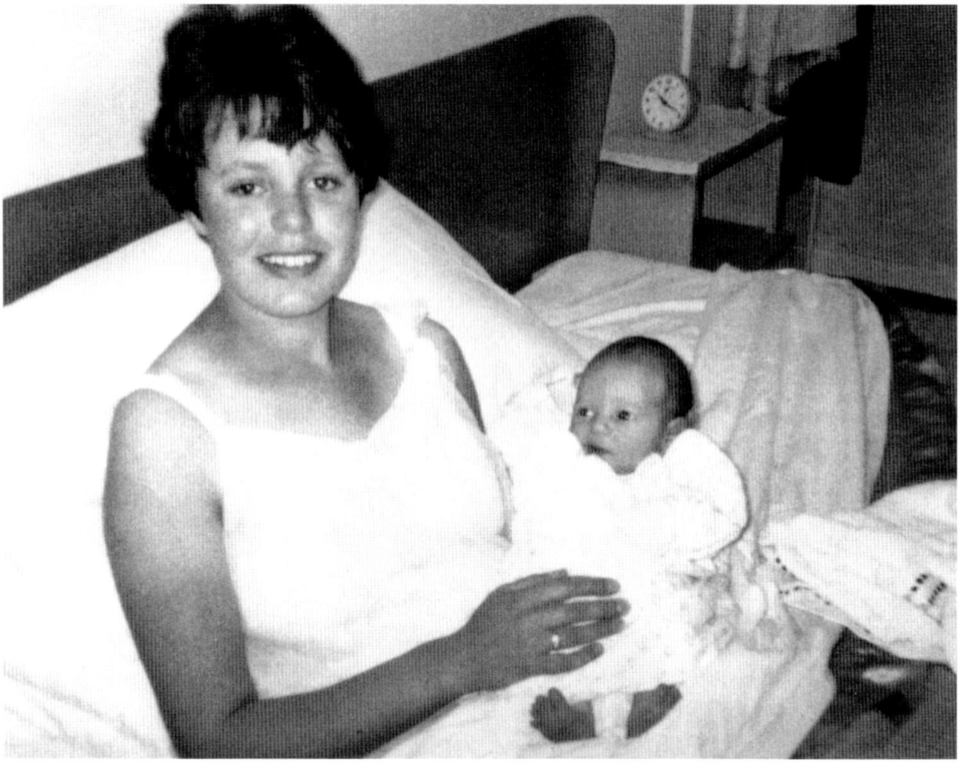

Above: A home birth. Pat Carter and baby Trevor. Home births were quite usual but a necessary stipulation was an inside toilet and bathroom, which was still not common to all homes. (Pat Carter)
Left: Trevor Carter, sitting in his pram. Babies were regularly put outside to get fresh air. Prams were often put at the bottom of the garden. It was quite common to let the babies 'cry for a bit until they settled down'. (Pat Carter)

For mothers who gave birth at home, a local midwife was on call. If an ambulance was needed, only minimal medical assistance was available from the driver; in the early sixties, ambulance drivers just needed basic first aid training and a clean driving licence. In August 1962, an ambulance arrived at the Brook Hospital in Woolwich to transfer a very sick baby to Hackney's Queen Elizabeth hospital. It was discovered that the incubator plug did not fit the ambulance socket. With siren blaring and blue light flashing, the ambulance sped from west to north London with the incubator swathed in blankets to keep the baby warm. A nurse and the baby's father took turns to hold up a life-saving drip attached to the baby's tiny ankle. It was not until later that electrical equipment in ambulances became uniformly compatible with hospital circuits. After 1965, ambulance services throughout the UK were upgraded and drivers were required to be medically trained to provide treatment as well as transport.

From its inception, the ever-expanding NHS suffered from acute staffing shortages and relied on immigrant workers to provide a steady supply of much needed labour. Immigrants, mainly from Ireland, Pakistan and the Caribbean, arrived throughout the sixties to train as doctors, nurses and midwives. The largest wave came from Jamaica. By the end of 1965 there were 3–5,000 Jamaican nurses in British hospitals, chiefly working in London and the Midlands.

As children grew, regular checks were available from Child Welfare clinics. Babies received free cod liver oil, malt extract and concentrated orange juice, rich in Vitamin C and D to help combat rickets – still prevalent in poorer communities. Throughout the decade, a growing school welfare system provided routine dental, eye and hearing tests examinations at age five, eleven and fourteen – as well as inspections for head lice by the 'nit nurse'. Young children received free milk at school, a third of a pint per child five days a week, to raise children's levels of Vitamin D. In cold winters, like 1962/3, it was common to see milk bottles outside school entrances with their silver bottle tops pushed up by columns of frozen milk, later often thawed out near classroom heaters.

The importance of children's health was regularly emphasised in parents' magazines. Advertisements for the latest baby and child care products in *Family Doctor* in 1964 included Marathon nappies,

'If you've always dreamed of becoming a nurse, here's your chance.' Nursing was a popular choice of career, particularly for young girls. (Janet Shepherd)

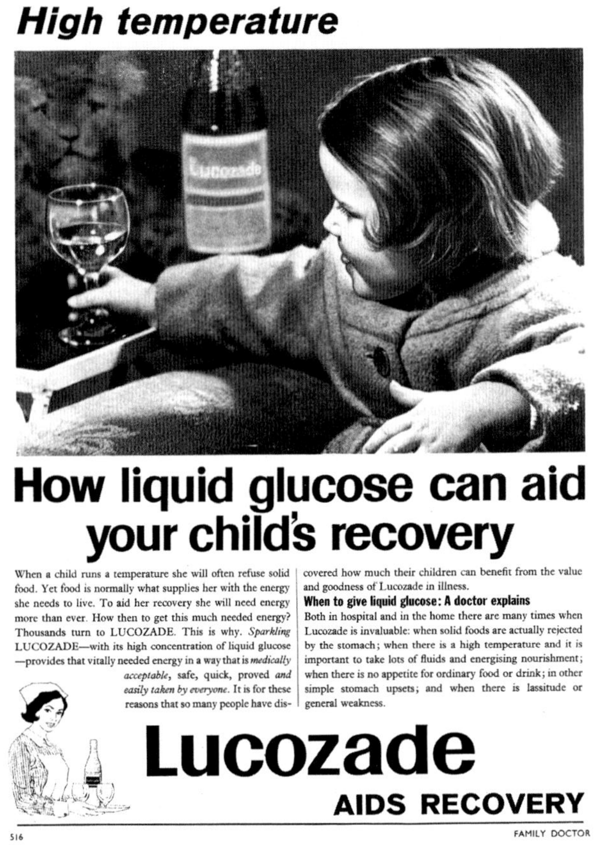

In the 1960s, Lucozade was advertised as a medicinal glucose syrup drink to provide energy for sick children and adults, especially when they were not allowed solid food. (Reproduced with the permission of Lucozade Ribena Suntory Ltd. All rights reserved)

Heinz and Cow & Gate baby foods, Lucozade, Pedigree prams, Lux mild soapflakes, plus Clarks and Start-Rite footwear.

Basic first aid treatments for children were found in most medicine cabinets. Iodine tincture, in small ridged blue glass bottles, that turned bright yellow and burned when applied, was used as an antiseptic for grazed knees and small wounds. Another staple was castor oil, generally regarded as unpleasant and used to treat constipation. Glass thermometers, with a mercury ball encased at one end and placed under the tongue, were regularly used but could be unsafe as children were known to bite through the end.

Respiratory illnesses, especially bronchitis, were endemic in some inner city areas like London's East End. Homes were often smoky because most heating, especially in poorer areas, came from coal fires. Even after the 1956 Clean Air Act, many people could not afford smokeless fuel. However, the biggest danger for millions of children came from adults smoking. Deaths from lung cancer had almost doubled in the 1950s and the number of people smoking continued to climb. This was despite Government health campaigns, a damning 1962 report from the Royal College of Physicians on *Smoking and Health* and, in 1965, the banning of cigarette advertising on television. *Family Doctor* started a Junior League of Non-Smokers, urging schools to create their own non-smoking groups, but the idea was not adopted nationally and petered out.

Although some of the worst childhood diseases had been eradicated, measles, mumps, German measles, chicken pox and tonsillitis were all still prevalent. The removal of a child's tonsils, usual in the 1950s, was less common due to a growing awareness of the danger to a child's immune system. Mass vaccination programmes were part of routine healthcare for children to prevent whooping cough, TB, smallpox, diphtheria and polio. Cases of polio

Bright scrapbook pictures showing a female nurse and a male doctor – acceptable gender stereotypes across the whole sixties decade.

A colourful and appealing tin of Dilly Duckling throat pastilles, specially designed to persuade children to suck lozenges to ease a sore throat. (Simpkins Sweets)

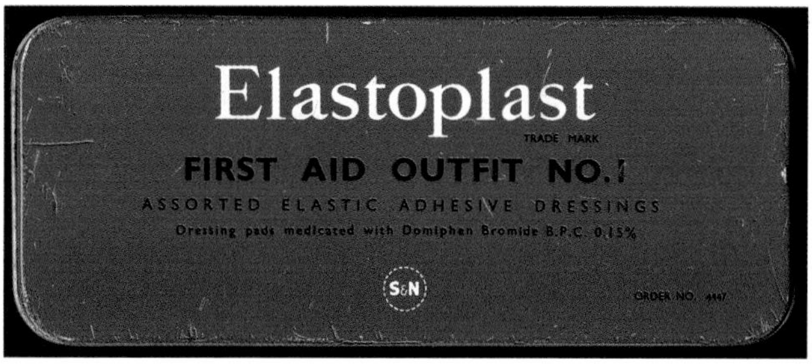

Plasters were sold in tins before the advent of plastic packaging. Children's grazed knees were commonly dabbed with iodine before a plaster was applied. Elastoplast was the brand leader for plasters. (Baiersdorf Health Care)

Above left: A young girl watches as she receives an inoculation in her arm. Vaccination was voluntary and, despite medical recommendations, not all parents allowed their children to receive a jab. (Mary Evans Picture Library)

Above right: A *Preliminary Home Nursing* booklet published by the St John Ambulance Association emphasised the importance of taking children to be inoculated against infectious diseases. (St John Ambulance; St John Ambulance is a volunteer-led charitable organisation dedicated to the teaching and practice of first aid)

fell dramatically when a live oral vaccine became memorably available on a sugar lump from 1962. A highly effective measles vaccine was introduced in 1968. However, although it produced a decline in the number of childhood deaths, there was insufficient take-up overall to stop the disease spreading throughout the seventies.

Many children had bad teeth, due to poor cleaning, excessive sugar and, in poorest families, a lack of Vitamin D and calcium. Routine dental work did not include much preventative work. Gas was still commonly used as an anaesthetic before tooth extractions. Many children were traumatised by having a black rubber mask pressed onto their face. Afterwards, the smell of the gas, dizziness and nausea could last for hours. It was a risky process that was later banned and replaced by a more routine use of injections. In an early advertisement for battery-operated toothbrushes, Ronson urged parents to purchase an automatic toothbrush: 'Spend 6 guineas [£6 6s] to save teeth ... by twelve, one out of four children will have lost second teeth, by twenty, one in ten people will have dentures.'

Did you know?

Medical science began to benefit from advances made in other scientific fields. Improvements in x-ray equipment owed a lot to photographic research, analgesics benefitted from advances in chemical engineering and the development of the transistor radio aided modern hearing aids.

Recreational drug taking became more widespread by the close of the decade. A growing teenage culture appeared to link 'pop' music and drugs, causing huge concern among the adult population. There was also a steady increase in prescribed drugs, for children as well as adults. In 2016, Sanchia Berg on the BBC 4 *Today* programme stated that in the 1960s, Home Office doctors gave the go-ahead for experimental drug trials on children at two approved schools. Disruptive boys at Richmond Hill Approved School in North Yorkshire 'were given anti-convulsant drugs to control their behaviour'. The issue of consent was left to school managers who said they saw 'no need to consult parents'.

Advances in health care and a range of new medicinal products, procedures and remedies enabled doctors to treat children more effectively, bringing enormous advances in the health of the nation's youth. By the end of the decade, it was recognised that parents had a right to be regularly informed, consulted and listened to over the medical treatment of their children.

'Better medicines for a better world': a 1960s advertisement from Parke-Davis, a medical firm specialising in modern pharmaceutical research, demonstrating advances over the centuries. (© Pfizer Inc)

4
Education

During the 1960s, British education underwent significant changes. The decade is memorable for progressive developments in the primary curriculum, the establishment of a comprehensive secondary school system and the creation of many new universities. The vast majority of children were educated in state schools with approximately only 9 per cent in private education and 1 per cent home schooled. Views on the decade's educational developments have polarised. For some it was a time of optimism and growth when state education provided greater opportunities while others believed that the changes had led to an erosion of standards.

For most of the decade, there was only minimal provision for nursery-age children. There were no state nursery schools and private provision was patchy. The seminal 1967 Plowden

A colourful *Look and Learn* magazine for junior school children, December 1962. *Look and Learn* merged with the long-running and more traditional *Children's Newspaper* in 1965.

Scrap pictures of children playing 'at school' with the boy as the teacher and the girl as the pupil. Many children owned a toy desk at home.

Jack and Jill Nursery class, 1968. The story of Little Black Sambo, featured on the wall, was later seen as racist and deemed unsuitable for school use. (Karen Livingstone)

Report, *Children and their Primary Schools,* highlighted the acute need for nursery schooling, especially in areas of social deprivation. It recommended that children over the age of three should have access to provision, whether in primary school nursery classes or in separate establishments. Following Plowden, 16,000 nursery places were therefore made available, but the post-war birth rate boom meant only around 10 per cent of children were able to secure a place by the end of the decade.

BBC Radio famously included a daily fifteen-minute slot for under-fives, *Listen with Mother,* throughout the 1950s and 1960s. It was a very popular programme for many young children and parents, well known for the adage, 'Are you sitting comfortably? Then I'll begin', which preceded the story. Later, BBC screened a television version, *Watch with Mother.*

Schooling for most children began the year they turned five, either in all-age primary schools for children aged five to eleven, or in separate Infant and Junior schools. The term 'Infants' was commonly used to refer to children aged between five and seven. The sign

'Middle Infants' school children (now termed Year One) wearing feather headdresses and singing North American Indian songs at an assembly for parents in 1967. (Debra Wade)

'Mixed Infants', often seen on former Victorian school buildings, indicated the modern entrance for young boys and girls, although their parents were rarely allowed past the school gates.

In the sixties, school buildings in some areas still lacked contemporary amenities. A 1960 Berkshire survey listed forty-five schools with earth closets and thirty-five with no mains water, while twenty-seven had open fires and six were lit by gas. In 1962, the Leeds Chief Education Officer George Taylor, in a *Guardian* article, highlighted the 'gulf between north and south' in living standards across England. He emphasised that nine county boroughs with the highest mortality rates were in the industrial North, while the ten lowest were in the South.

In the early sixties, junior schooling, from the age of seven, remained largely formal. The teacher stood at the front of the class and even young children were seated in desks. The 3Rs were given priority, times tables were chanted and poems learned by heart. Discipline could be strict, with some teachers employing corporal punishment. Alan Johnson remembers being caned by his primary school teacher: 'I wish I could remember why, but I struggle to come up with a single significant transgression.'

Primary classes were large, often with over thirty children taught by one teacher. Great importance was placed on daily handwriting practice. Nature study was commonly the only science and was taught informally; class nature tables typically contained random natural objects brought for display and later used in art lessons. In 1964, Granada Television began their famous documentary *Up* series to document the lives of fourteen seven-year-old children from different backgrounds to discover how social class affected life chances. They were subsequently televised every seven years. However, gender was not taken into account. Of the fourteen children, only four of the group were girls.

A quartet of carol singers: four six-year-old girls sing 'Silent Night' in an infant school Christmas concert in 1969. (Debra Wade)

Children present a traditional Nativity Play for parents in the early 1960s. Costumes were nearly always made by parents and rarely purchased or provided by the school. (Janet Shepherd)

Two large 1960s classes, each with thirty-six children. *Top photo*: a Glasgow school where most of the children are in school uniform. *Bottom photo*: a Northumberland school with children in their own clothes. (Janet Shepherd and Margaret Heppell)

By the late 1960s, the Plowden Report introduced a sea change in primary education. A plethora of new ideas focussed on 'child centred learning, discovery methods, creativity and spontaneity'. Teachers began to experiment with progressive teaching methods. Rows of desks were replaced by informal groups of tables. Children were encouraged to work

A girl in an infant school classroom uses graded wooden Cuisenaire rods to help develop mathematical concepts, *c.* 1965. The rods came in ten colours, and were graded from 1 to 10 cm in length. They were still used in some classrooms in 2018. (Mary Evans Picture Library)

individually and there was far less whole class teaching. Some open-plan schools encouraged team teaching; the best known was Prior Weston, in London's Barbican, under its head teacher, Henry Pluckrose. Opened in 1968, the school fostered creativity and individuality. Unusually, Henry regularly taught classes himself. The school was noted for art, poetry, music and drama and became internationally famous. By the close of the sixties, John Holt's book *How Children Fail* (1964), an indictment of traditional teaching methods, became a best seller.

Reading schemes, like Janet and John, were replaced with modern equivalents. Ladybird's new Keywords series famously featured Peter and Jane. Sheila McCullough's One Two Three and Away series, published by Collins, lasted into the 1980s. There was a belief that learning to read could be acquired by memorising whole words and teaching phonics fell out of favour. Some schools experimented with the Initial Teaching Alphabet (ITA) – created by Sir James Pitman, grandson of Sir Isaac Pitman who invented shorthand. It was purportedly a simpler way to teach children to read and write than using the traditional alphabet. At age seven, children transferred to orthodox spelling but problems with the transition led to the scheme falling into disfavour.

Primary school children often listened to radio programmes, like *Music, Mime and Movement* and *Singing Together*. For drama and 'physical training' (PT) most children exercised in vests, pants and either bare feet or black plimsolls, 'pumps', often cheaply available in Woolworths. Primary school uniform was often informal but generally boys wore short trousers, only changing to long trousers at secondary school. Drama and music featured at Stephen Wade's working-class London primary school, where his top junior class staged an ambitious production of *A Midsummer Night's Dream*. Each child had a part and the parents made all the costumes.

Above: A group of junior school boys and girls work together to make various items for a class project on Switzerland. (Margaret Heppell)
Below: Excited children from a mixed junior school class, wearing their own clothes, on a day trip to the countryside in the mid-1960s. (Margaret Heppell)

Above left: The Initial Teaching Alphabet or ITA was introduced in some schools as a better way to teach children to read and write. It included fourteen extra symbols for double sounds.
Above right: *The Racing Car Mystery*, a book from Hulton's Adventure Road to Reading junior school series targeted at boys. Gender bias was common in 1960s reading schemes.

A BBC Radio *Singing Together* booklet, autumn 1966. The weekly broadcasts mainly featured traditional British folk songs and rhymes, but also some international melodies. (BBC Radio For Schools)

Did you know?

'Let's bring Noddy Back from Exile!' A 1968 *Daily Mail* article urged schools and libraries to lift the ban on children's author, Enid Blyton, for 'colour prejudice, limited vocabulary and middle-class bias'. The paper wanted censorship removed from Blyton who 'ranked alongside Stalin and Lenin in the best-seller lists'.

In 1944, the Butler Education Act had established free secondary education for all, based on a variety of schools to suit different aptitudes and abilities. Initially a tri-partite system of grammar, technical and secondary modern schools was envisaged. However, by the sixties most children attended either grammar or modern schools (known as secondary moderns) and there were often regional variations in the provision of school places. Testing at ten to eleven years was considered the most effective way to discover which type of education a child was best suited to. Accordingly, in their final primary school year, most children sat an eleven-plus examination in arithmetic, spelling, composition and, most crucially, 'Intelligence Papers' to determine IQ levels. The highest achieving top quarter went to grammar schools while the remaining three quarters were placed in secondary moderns. Although not the intention, in practice the eleven-plus became seen as a pass/fail exam. The style and content of the examination also tended to favour middle class children over those from working class backgrounds.

Secondary moderns were originally intended to provide pupils aged eleven to fifteen (school leaving age was fifteen until 1972) with training in a 'wide range of simple, practical skills', such as basic English and Arithmetic, woodworking and cookery. Implementation was left to local authorities but overall there were minimal opportunities for academic study. One pupil recalled, 'We were condemned to a lifetime of exclusion

Junior schools gradually began to introduce simple science experiments: 'a jam jar, milk bottle top, knitting needle and a match was all that was needed for a flotation experiment'. (Janet Shepherd)

A secondary modern school report for the spring term, 1962. Comments by teachers tended to be brief and repetitive. In the days before computers, all school reports were handwritten by different members of staff – a lengthy process. (Janet Shepherd)

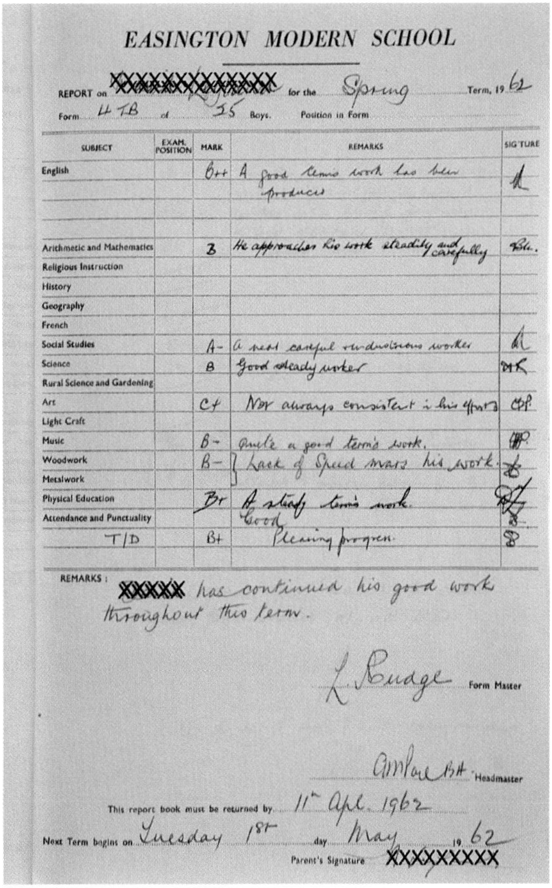

EASINGTON MODERN SCHOOL

REPORT on [redacted] for the Spring Term, 1962
Form 4 TB of 35 Boys. Position in Form

SUBJECT	EXAM. POSITION	MARK	REMARKS	SIG'TURE
English		B+	A good term's work has been produced	[illegible]
Arithmetic and Mathematics		B	He approaches his work steadily and carefully	[illegible]
Religious Instruction				
History				
Geography				
French				
Social Studies		A-	A neat careful industrious worker	[illegible]
Science		B	Good steady worker	[illegible]
Rural Science and Gardening				
Art		C+	Not always consistent in his efforts	[illegible]
Light Craft				
Music		B-	Quite a good term's work.	[illegible]
Woodwork		B-	Lack of Speed mars his work.	[illegible]
Metalwork				
Physical Education		B+	A steady term's work.	[illegible]
Attendance and Punctuality			Good	[illegible]
T/D		B+	Pleasing progress.	[illegible]

REMARKS: [redacted] has continued his good work throughout this term.

L. Rudge Form Master

[illegible] B.A. Headmaster

This report book must be returned by 11th Apl. 1962

Next Term begins on Tuesday 1st day May 1962

Parent's Signature [redacted]

and crippling self-doubt ... they weren't pleasant places to be if you were into art or books...' Many secondary modern schools gave no opportunities for children to obtain qualifications. Some more progressive schools encouraged abler pupils to sit certain General Certificate in Education (GCE) Ordinary level subjects (O levels) but not Advanced levels. Pupils who achieved comparable O level grades to grammar students were rarely permitted to switch schools and study at a higher level. From 1965, a new Certificate in Secondary Education (CSE) provided a means for less academic children to achieve qualifications but did little to reduce the gulf between secondary moderns and grammars. By 1960, there was much criticism of the limited syllabus on offer in most secondary modern schools and the failure to adequately equip children for the world of work. The 1963 Newsom Report, *Half Our Future*, urged that secondary modern pupils should receive a far greater share of educational resources.

In contrast, grammar schools, established for generations as academically oriented institutions, were accorded prestige by both the educational community and the general public. The top 25 per cent of children were selected by the eleven-plus for a grammar school education. It was argued that this selective system provided a route for bright working class children to obtain academic schooling. In practice, grammar schools attracted a disproportionately high number of middle class children and arguably disadvantaged the working class child. Many working class children and parents felt alienated by the grammar school ethos. High scholastic expectations often went hand in hand with strict discipline and dress codes. Image was all important; smart grammar school blazers and ties, caps or berets, were common for both boys and girls.

By 1960, a growing body of educational opinion thought selection at eleven was divisive and that most secondary modern pupils received a second class education. This led to the introduction of a non-selective comprehensive system, signalling the end of the eleven-plus

Some secondary schools had strong music departments. Hendon County Grammar School choir recorded traditional folk songs with English bass singer Owen Brannigan in 1964. It was digitally remastered in 1989.

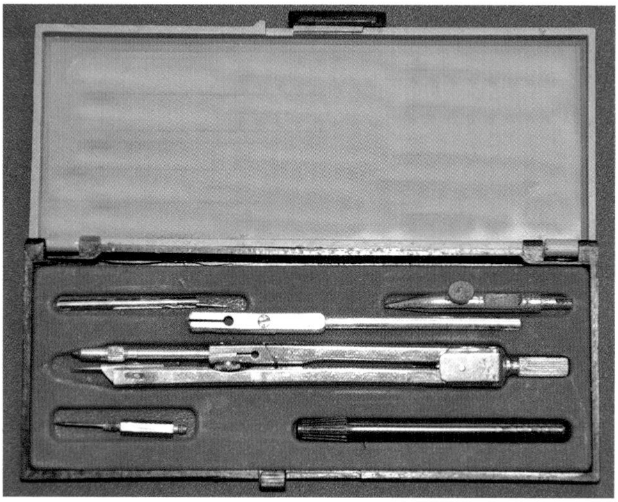

Geometry and algebra were rarely taught until secondary school level. A school compass set from 1960s in a new-style plastic box. (Janet Shepherd)

examination. The new comprehensive schools catered for 'all abilities and aptitudes' in a local catchment area. It was considered that this egalitarian system would produce a better educated workforce and in turn facilitate economic growth.

Comprehensive schools could vary, from borough to borough and school to school. Some took children from eleven to fifteen years, others to eighteen. The early comprehensive years often comprised a diagnostic stage, with subject specialisation introduced only later. One example of three different Inner London Education Authority (ILEA) comprehensive schools was in North London. Risinghill opened in 1960 under its radical head teacher, Michael Duane, who was an advocate of progressive and non-authoritarian schooling. His policies led to media criticism and disputes with the local authority. However, falling rolls led to the school being compulsorily closed in 1965. It was later immortalised in Leila Berg's *Risinghill: Death of a Comprehensive* (1968). Another comprehensive, Highbury Grove, was run from 1967 by its head teacher, Rhodes Boyson, as a traditional grammar school, with strict discipline and a competitive house system. Boyson later became a Conservative MP and one of a group of right-wing educators and writers who produced a series of 'Black Papers' from 1969 criticising both the comprehensive system and the 'excesses' of progressive education. These academics argued for the retention of the eleven-plus examination and traditional teaching methods. A third school, Woodberry Down Comprehensive, built on a large London council estate in 1954, flourished by the 1960s as a co-educational eleven to eighteen comprehensive under head teacher Harriet Chetwyn. The school successfully attracted students from further afield as well as local pupils.

After 1965, comprehensive organisation rapidly expanded when the Labour Government compulsorily instructed LEAs to implement the new system. The pace of change was very rapid. Between 1965 and 1975, 90 per cent of English secondary schools turned comprehensive. However, a fully comprehensive system was never achieved and around 160 grammar schools survived.

Did you know?

'A new *Top of the Form*'. For the first time, in 1964, the traditional radio quiz programme for secondary schools, *Top of the Form*, allowed mixed teams of girls and boys to compete and additionally opened the competition to teams from comprehensive schools.

Children with mental and physical disabilities were placed in special schools according to their needs. The largest group were those classified as educationally sub-normal (ESN), a 'catch-all' category that removed children with below average IQs out of mainstream schools. Doctors' certificates could be used to coerce non-compliant parents into agreement. Although some mildly disabled children were educated in mainstream schools, they were a minority.

A class of mixed teenage students work together in a large classroom at Holland Park Comprehensive School, London, in 1965. Holland Park school opened in 1958 and became a flagship for comprehensive education in the 1960s. (Mary Evans Picture Library)

'An apple for the teacher' – one of a set of six 'tongue in cheek' badges issued in bubble gum vending machines in the 1960s. Others included 'Down with Homework' and 'Offishall Spelling Champ' (*sic*).

Those with the severest learning difficulties were classified as 'severely subnormal' (SSN) and deemed 'ineducable'. Later in the decade, the curriculum began to be adapted to an individual child's needs. Some progress towards integrating special needs children into ordinary schools began, but their education largely remained unchanged until the late 1970s.

During the 1960s, schools played an important role in the education of increasing numbers of migrant children and in promoting community cohesion. Later in the decade, many local authorities, like ILEA, developed multi-cultural equal opportunities policies and practices together with more in-service programmes.

In the early sixties, fewer than 5 per cent of young people went to university, and of these under a quarter were women. The 1963 Robbins report advocated a massive extension and widening of opportunities in higher education. New modern 'plate glass' universities, most notably East Anglia, Essex, Kent, Lancaster, Warwick and York, were created. Where previously universities had been predominantly male institutions, an increasing number of women were accepted onto degree courses. In April 1965, Cabinet minister Tony Crosland's notable 'Woolwich Speech' led to another major change in education with the establishment of polytechnic establishments alongside universities. Opportunities for study were further extended when the distance-learning Open University (OU) was created in 1969 to widen adult access to higher education in particular. The OU, based at Walton Hall, close to the new city of Milton Keynes, will celebrate its golden anniversary in 2019.

The decade saw key developments in teacher training. In 1960, courses were extended from two to three years and in-service training became obligatory. Training colleges evolved into Colleges of Education and some combined with polytechnics. In the later sixties, there was a huge increase in the numbers entering teacher training. A four-year course, leading to a Bachelor of Education degree, was established with the first BEd students graduating in 1968. A campaign to persuade married women to return to teaching was launched in 1961 and by 1965 nursery classes were established for teachers' children to encourage more women back into the profession. Sidney Webb College of Education, established in 1961 in London's West End, was a notable institution which provided unique day and evening teacher training courses for adult mature students, particularly women.

The sweeping changes implemented in the 1960s were regarded by some as too radical. Liberal educationists were criticised for discarding traditional methods of teaching and learning. Others believed the new educational reforms in the 1960s brought greater depth and better social equality into the nation's educational system.

5
Teenage Culture

By the mid-sixties, the younger generation viewed the world very differently from their parents. Teenagers were more outspoken, far less respectful of established authority and willing to protest against seeming injustices. The English rock band The Who's song 'My Generation' contained the memorable line 'I hope to die before I get old', which came to epitomise teenage angst. The American actor James Dean, who had died a decade earlier, remained a 'cult icon of teenage disillusionment'. However, the voices of youth were not all negative. Young people across the world openly supported the US Civil Rights movement and campaigned for nuclear disarmament and for women's rights. Fulltime work for school leavers, 'Saturday jobs' and paper rounds for pupils and students were plentiful. Teenagers became the new consumers, spending their money mostly on music and fashion. A popular, 'pop', culture was noticeable from the mid-sixties, with the onset of 'Beatlemania', pirate radio stations and the arrival of Mary Quant's fashion revolution. A downside was conflict between different youth groups, the steady rise in drug use across the decade and the growing divide between the generations.

The 1960s was a time of musical creativity and innovation. From 1963, ITV's Friday night programme *Ready Steady Go!* embodied the spirit of British pop music. It was 'our bible ... the show we would not miss'. Presenter Cathy McGowan, herself a teenager, soon became known as the 'face of youth'. British singers Adam Faith and Cliff Richard received top billing and many songs broadcast on the show shot straight to number one in the charts. On most Saturday mornings in 1963, up to a million fans might rush out and buy the top number one hit on a 'single', a small 45 rpm vinyl record, after watching *Ready Steady Go!*.

John Shepherd, age eighteen, at home in 1960, practising how to play 'Peggy Sue' by Buddy Holly on his new Spanish guitar. (John Shepherd)

The changing teenage years. A thirteen-year-old girl in school uniform in 1960 and the same girl photographed four years later. (Janet Shepherd)

A mixed group of teenagers in a summer garden. Note the trumpet, the waistcoat and the Vespa scooter – 'not just a scooter but a way of life'. (Janet Shepherd)

Between 1964 and 1967, popular music was celebrated on pirate radio stations like Radio Caroline and Radio London. They broadcast to huge audiences twenty-four hours a day, transmitting from off-shore ships in the North Sea and eclipsing the BBC's daily offering of just forty-five minutes of 'pop'. Later, the BBC launched their highly successful new station Radio One in 1967, with DJ Tony Blackburn playing songs by the Bee Gees and Tremeloes. One of Radio One's other early presenters was a young Noel Edmonds.

Early 1960s pop music provoked negative reactions from many adults and even from some children. 'Unpleasant noise,' one boy wrote to the *Eagle* comic. Most young people disagreed. In January 1961, ten-year-old Alan Johnson proudly knew that 'number one in the Top Twenty' was 'Poetry in Motion' by Johnny Tillotson. Stephen Wade remembers his family getting a free portable record player by saving Green Shield Stamps, issued to their

Above left: Pop music was mainly produced on small 45 rpm vinyl records – 'singles'. 'A Teenager in Love' is regarded as one of the greatest songs in rock and roll history. Marty Wilde's version remained popular throughout the sixties. (Reproduced with Permission of Philips)
Above right: Cut-out pictures of two young sixties teenagers making music with a guitar and recorder. A typical 1960s standard lamp stands in the background.
Right: Two of the 'Fab Four': Beatles John Lennon and George Harrison on their USA tour, 1964. John was murdered in New York, aged forty, on 8 December 1980. (Mary Evans Picture Library)

customers by many local shops. The first record Stephen bought was *Happy Together* by the Turtles. He recalls *The Zodiac: Cosmic Sounds* being played in his school music lesson and wanting the whole album. His mother searched through many record shops before finding this 'cult classic' with its psychedelic record sleeve and twelve separate tracks, one for each astrological sign. Gradually, the popular music so espoused by teenagers began to be taken more seriously. In 1965, the *Observer* appointed George Melly as its first 'critic of pop culture' to persuade classical music lovers that 'Bob Dylan and Dr Who were worth a look too'.

It was the Beatles phenomenon that transformed the pop music world. All four boys were from Liverpool, part of that city's highly creative pop generation. From the moment John Lennon, Paul McCartney, George Harrison and 'Ringo' Starr started playing together, a legend was born. With their talent, drive and determination, the Beatles became 'rock royalty', not only in Liverpool and the UK, but across the world. On 22 March 1963, their first number one album, *Please Please Me*, was issued, marking the start of 'Beatlemania'. The group's pre-eminence was unchallenged and they took America by storm in their 1964 tour of the States. The same year, Stephen's mother took him to see the Beatles' first film, *A Hard Day's Night*, in London's Old Kent Road. 'The queue stretched back over Canal Bridge. We waited for two hours as the cinema was full and we had to queue for the next showing but it was worth it. The Beatles were everything just then.' The *New Musical Express* declared: 'In the distant future, our descendants ... will see one word printed against the year 1963 – Beatles!'

Did you know?

On November 1963, 200 girls from an Accrington cotton mill went on strike when their foreman banned them from listening to the very popular morning radio programme *Housewives' Choice*. He complained they were liable to scream when they heard the Beatles sing and then lost interest in their work.

Sally Martin with her Beatles-style guitar in around 1964. 'Beatlemania' was rampant by the mid-sixties and young children as well as teenagers were aware of the group's popularity and success. (Sally Jones)

The Beatles' unique music, together with their choice of an alternative 'hippie' lifestyle of 'peace not war', influenced a generation. John Lennon's 'Give Peace a Chance', released in 1969, became an anthem for peace movements across the globe. In Britain, teenagers flocked to join peace campaigns like the Campaign for Nuclear Disarmament (CND).

Sixties Merseyside music did not only produce the Beatles but other notable groups such as Gerry and the Pacemakers and the Searchers. Elsewhere, London bands like The Who, The Rolling Stones and The Kinks also hit the headlines; the latter two groups were arguably the most talented ones after the Beatles. Just a few years earlier, solo artist Cliff Richard had dominated the British pop charts, eventually becoming the third top selling artist in the UK behind the Beatles and Elvis Presley. Most pop songs were vocals, but the Tornados topped the singles chart with 'Telstar', one of the first sci-fi influenced pop songs, named after the USA's Telstar communications satellite, launched in July 1962. In 1967, a young Sandie Shaw memorably became the first British entrant to win the Eurovision Song contest with 'Puppet on a String'.

Did you know?

In 1961, aged fifteen, pop singer Helen Shapiro topped the hit parade twice with 'Walking Back to Happiness' and 'You Don't Know'. She became 'Britain's Top Female Singer' and remains the youngest female artist to have reached number one in charts. In early 1963, the Beatles appeared as one of her supporting acts. Helen's family did not own a record player, so she listened to her first hit on a neighbour's machine.

The year the Beatles hit stardom, Cliff Richard starred in the hugely successful 1963 musical *Summer Holiday*. Musicals, especially from America, appealed to the British public. Music from *South Pacific* had forty-six weeks at number one on the charts, even eclipsing the Beatles' 'Please Please Me'. Two West End musicals loved by young and old alike were *Oliver!*, later made into a hugely successful 1968 film, and *Fiddler on the Roof*, running at London's Her Majesty's Theatre in 1967 for over 2,000 performances. *The Sound of Music* soundtrack was in the Top Ten chart for five years; by 1968 it had sold more than 2 million copies in Britain alone. Humorous songs appealed to adults and children, e.g. Lonnie Donnegan's 'My Old Man's a Dustman', Peter Sellers and Sophia Loren with 'Goodness Gracious Me' and the hilarious 'Hole in the Road', sung by the well-known English actor Bernard Cribbins.

In February 1962, *The Sunday Times*'s first colour supplement featured images of a young girl in a grey flannel dress, Jean

Theatre programme, *Fiddler on the Roof*, 5 June 1967. West End musicals attracted adults, teenagers and children. Jewish actor Topol apologised for being unavailable for this performance – he was in Israel following the outbreak of the Six Day War.

Above left: 'Take Three Girls'. Three young girls cross the street wearing miniskirts, Trafalgar Square, London. A number 11 bus heading to Liverpool Street passes in the background. (Mary Evans Picture Library)
Above right: Dolls' fashion often replicated real life. A colourful 1960s postcard with three dolls dressed in different modern outfits. Long white socks were often worn with short dresses or skirts.

Shrimpton. The photos were taken by the fashion photographer David Bailey and the dress designer was the British fashion guru Mary Quant. Shrimpton, with another model, Lesley Lawson, better known as 'Twiggy', became emblematic of 'Swinging London' and fashion icons for teenage girls.

Mary Quant is forever associated with the introduction of the miniskirt. She promoted 'fun fashion' for sixties youth, including 'hot-pants, go-go boots and space age tunics'. Quant famously sported the geometric hairstyle created by stylist Vidal Sassoon, known as the 'bob cut', or 'the shape'. Its straight lines represented a complete change from the curling and crimping hairstyles of the fifties. Sixties fashion was inextricably associated with the growth of Carnaby Street in London's Soho. This cosmopolitan area hit the headlines on 15 April 1966 when the front cover of the US *Time* magazine extolled the street's colourful clothes and fashionable boutiques, describing London as the 'swinging city'.

Did you know?

'Taxman to take a cut from the Mini-Skirt'. Skirts shorter than 24 inches (61 cm) were classed as children's wear and not taxed. However, with so many adults purchasing 'little girl-look' miniskirts, the Exchequer announced that from 1 November 1968 only skirts below 20 inches would be exempt. Bradford *Telegraph & Argus*, 1968.

Sixties teenagers were the first youthful generation with money to spend on fashionable clothing. Although most youngsters could not afford Carnaby Street creations, many copies appeared in high street shops: 'mini and maxi skirts, hot pants, corduroys, snazzy shirts, cravats...' Space age fashion was epitomised by high gleaming boots and goggle-style sun glasses. PVC arrived, 'that super shiny man-made stuff'. Modern cosmetics could be purchased cheaply on the high street. In the early 1960s, Rimmel's 'Beauty on a Budget' range was launched as 'All that's best for beauty, at 1/3*d*' (about 15p). The preference was for dark eye make-up; mascara came in a block to be moistened, often with spit, before brushing it on. One popular 1961 song was 'War Paint', by the English pop duo the Brook Brothers:

> In your lipstick, powder and paint,
> All dressed up like what you ain't,
> You dye your hair a different shade,
> We're going to a movie not a masquerade.

Woolworths sold low-priced jewellery with dangling clip, or screw-on, ear rings. Pointed stiletto shoes were all the rage, although from 1963, the 'Mod' look was 'granny' shoes with stumpy heels. Over the decade, clothes gradually became less formal, with denim jeans the default choice for many young people. Girls elected for shorter hairstyles while boys preferred longer hair, a reversal of previous norms; schoolboy Stephen remembers wearing his hair long in direct opposition to the rules at his grammar school.

The nation's youth rejected traditional ballroom dancing in favour of dances like The Twist, a worldwide disco craze made famous in 1960 by American singer Chubby Checker. For pupils, occasional school dances were held, under teachers' supervision. Girls would sit on one side of the school hall, boys on the other, with only the bravest boys crossing the room to ask a girl to dance. It was very different from America with its adult-style 'high school proms'; dating in 1960s Britain usually comprised a trip to the cinema or maybe a coffee bar. At home, teenagers customised their bedrooms with photographs of favourite pop or film stars. The growth of central heating meant that bedrooms became better utilised. Youngsters sprawled on beds, played vinyl discs on Dansette record players and listened to pirate radio

A teenage girl feeling a bit out of place at a formal ball. Full-skirted dresses worn with high heels were popular. (Janet Shepherd)

stations on new transistor radios. For those whose parents could afford them, audio compact cassette players arrived, becoming the sought-after product for older children and teenagers.

When National Service ceased in December 1960, the 'schooling' previous generations had received from two years in the armed forces became a thing of the past. Afterwards, young boys leaving school either went straight into the workplace or higher education. Many adults deplored the ending of National Service and fears were voiced over 'teenage delinquency'. Their views were confirmed when two conflicting youth subcultures, commonly known as 'Mods and Rockers', hit the headlines. 'Rockers' favoured motor bikes and rock and roll music. Their 'teddy boy' fashion harked back to the Edwardian era, with velvet collared jackets and drainpipe trousers. 'Mods' preferred scooters, rhythm and blues music, tight fitting shirts and denim jeans. Mods and Rockers memorably clashed violently in the seaside towns of Clacton, Hastings and Brighton during Easter 1964. Media coverage was heavily condemnatory, denigrating a youth culture with 'no respect for authority'. It sparked nationwide concerns and almost moral panic amid calls for the return of National Service.

The clash between Mods and Rockers on British beaches was reportedly drug-fuelled. Recreational drug use among the young increasingly worried the adult generation. Despite regular price increases, amphetamines, or 'purple hearts', and barbiturate pills were swallowed by a growing number of youngsters while cocaine and heroin use increased ten-fold during the sixties. Alternative 'hippie' lifestyles tended towards a drug culture. Drugs were openly taken by the Beatles. 'Sgt Pepper's Lonely Hearts Club Band', released in 1967, was an example that was 'full of veiled references'. Shocking revelations were aired concerning the popular TV series for young children, *The Magic Roundabout*, which purportedly had undertones of 'drug use, hallucinogenic imagery and sexual innuendo'.

The 1960s has been termed the 'decade that shook Britain', the era of 'sex, pop and drugs'. The contraceptive pill brought youngsters a new sexual freedom, regarded as promiscuity by their elders, and an ever widening chasm developed between the generations. Sixties teenagers were assertive, confident and forward-looking, striving to portray a distinctive culture from that of their parents. They were the 'baby boomers', now viewed as the twentieth century's most fortunate generation.

Women often married earlier in the 1960s. Teenage bride Pat Carter with new husband Graham leave their wedding reception in an Austin Princess car, 22 July 1961. Pat's dress was made from Nottingham witchcraft lace by her Auntie Queenie. (Pat Carter)

6
Toys, Science and Technology

The sixties was a time of change and expansion in the toy industry. In 1960, two thirds of all toys were made of metal; ten years later, metal had largely been replaced by plastic. Gender differences gradually lessened as the decade progressed. To start with, toys for boys were soldiers, 'cowboy and American Indian' figures, cars and guns, while girls were given traditional baby dolls and dolls' houses. By the late sixties, the most sought-after toys were those associated with recent scientific and technological developments, science fiction and the race to conquer space. The decade also saw the growth of a more educational approach to toy design.

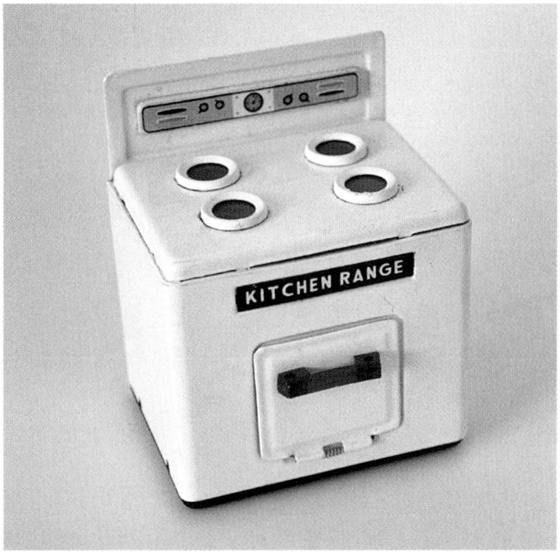

A metal doll's house Kitchen Range cooker from the early 1960s with four rings, a pull-down door and a dashboard timer.

1960s wooden bricks in a small truck on wheels. Many babies learned to walk pushing larger versions known as 'baby walkers'.

Colourful wooden hanging silhouettes in the sixties often featured favourite fairy tales such as 'Snow White and the Seven Dwarfs'.

Small plastic toys usually found in Christmas crackers often had small loops so they could be attached onto bracelets.

In 1961, the British Standards Institute introduced stringent regulations banning lead paint and restricting the use of celluloid and toxic dyes. Most toy firms ceased to use metal and turned exclusively to 'colourful, hardwearing, inexpensive' plastic. Forward-looking toy firms like Galt & Co. urged designers and manufacturers to consider the work of child psychologists and educators like Froebel and Montessori. By the late 1960s, anti-war sentiments had turned public taste away from military toys.

Science and space travel began to influence the British toy market from the 1950s. The radio science fiction programme *Journey into Space* (1953–8) had many devoted child listeners while 'Dan Dare Pilot of the Future' was the focal series in *Eagle*, the foremost boys' comic. Fortunate children watched on television as the Soviet Union's Sputnik satellite took off in 1957 and the first space astronaut, Yuri Gagarin, was launched into space in 1961. Memorably, children and adults across the world witnessed film of the first moon landing in 1969.

Notable advances in science provided major marketing opportunities for the toy industry to exploit scientific progress and also foster curiosity among the young. Museums, like

London's notable Science Museum, held well-attended exhibitions, with space-related toys becoming 'must-haves', although marketing was chiefly gender-biased and prioritised boys. In 1961, *Spacewar!* was one of the earliest digital computer games. Moon mission board games, toy rockets, satellites, space colouring books, jigsaws and a friction-powered Gemini capsule all appeared in the shops. As the space race between the USSR and the USA accelerated, science fiction was overtaken by real life. The intensive media coverage had an impact on *Blue Peter* fan Mark Dunton, who fantasised he could build 'a fully functioning rocket out of empty baked bean tins'.

Toy manufacturers were quick to capitalise on the popularity of television's *Doctor Who*. Blue telephone boxes and toy metal Daleks screaming 'Exterminate! Exterminate!' reached the toy shops. *Stingray* and *Thunderbirds* were two other science fiction series for children, starring puppets rather than people. Pelham Puppets produced *Thunderbirds* puppets while Dinky secured the rights to make *Thunderbird* vehicles. Mark thought *Thunderbirds* was ahead of its time: 'Its creator, Gerry Anderson, understood that little boys loved destruction and explosions and produced brilliant side-effects.'

Some other science toys encouraged exploration of the natural world. Both parents and teachers saw a greater need for science literacy. Sophisticated magnifying glasses and toy microscopes appeared alongside up-to-date chemistry sets. In 1960, Skil Craft Biology Lab sold a toolkit for investigating plants and animals and the popularity of photographic slides led to camera projectors being produced for children. Confectioners were also quick to exploit the enthusiasm for new scientific and technological developments. Children could buy 'Space Patrol Sweet Cigarettes' or 'Sky Ray' and 'Zoom' lollipops.

Toys reflected changes at home. Suburban house developments were replicated in building sets like 'Build-A-Home' or 'Betta Builda', with some constructions resembling 1960s high rise blocks. The continuing popularity of Hollywood Western films led to yet more toy guns, holsters, studded belts, cowboy hats and 'Wild West' clothes. Quaker introduced Puffed Wheat as their new 'shot from guns' breakfast cereal.

The growth of the modern car industry was reflected in toy vehicles. In 1961, Lesney Toys released their first Matchbox King model to be fitted with plastic windows. Petrol companies attracted new customers by offering free gifts for children as well as adults. Esso's 'Put a Tiger in your Tank' campaign offered free badges, imitation 'tiger tails' and 'tiger mugs' with petrol purchases.

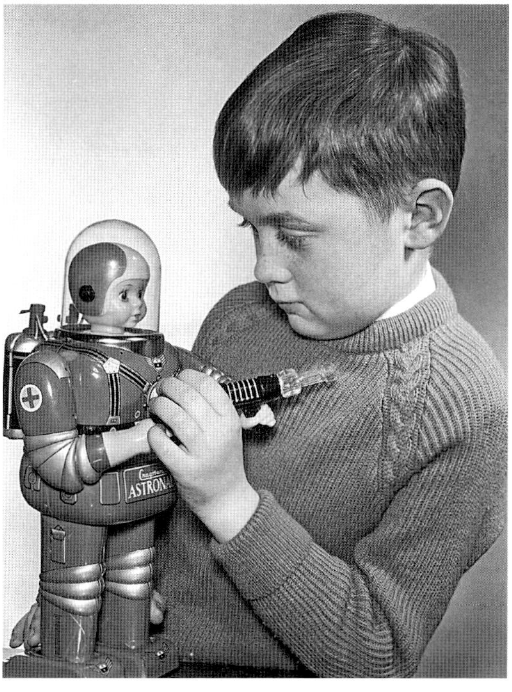

A boy with his toy astronaut, early 1960s. Space toys were hugely popular and included robots, rockets, space guns and spaceships as well as astronauts. (Mary Evans Picture Library)

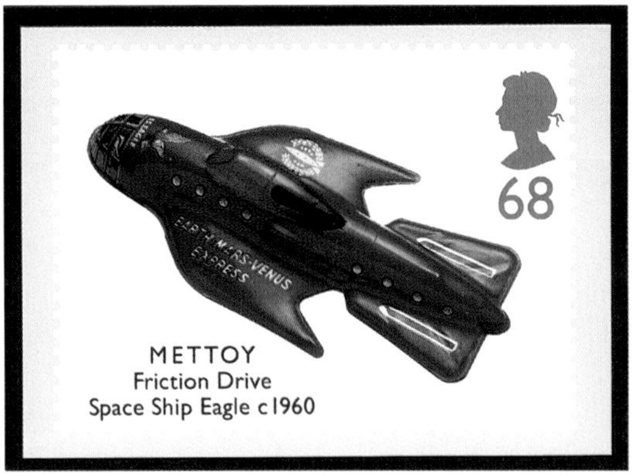

A bright red 'Earth-Mars-Venus' Express Rocket – a friction drive space ship toy rocket on sale in the 1960s, here featured on a Royal Mail stamp from 2003. (Stamp designs © Royal Mail Group Ltd)

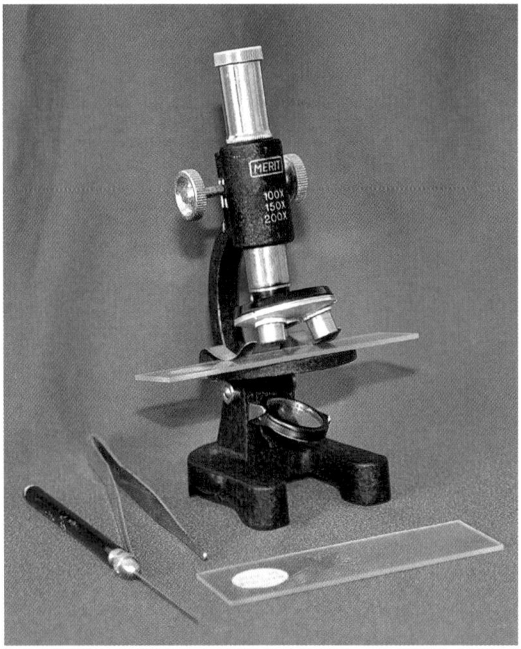

More accurate science toys began to appear in good toy shops. This is a child's working toy microscope, complete with tools and a set of glass slides.

The race to put the first man on the moon led to products with a space theme becoming all the rage, even extending to children's sweets. (Robert Opie Collections)

Small colourful scrap pictures of two children playing 'Cowboys and Indians'. The game derived from Hollywood Western films. Boys were always the chiefs and the girls were the squaws.

A toy red Routemaster London bus. The Routemaster became the best known of all the London buses and was specifically designed for service in the capital. (Meccano)

A toy Volkswagen camper van. Camper vans were popular throughout the decade for family camping at home and, increasingly, abroad.

Did you know?

A unique 1962 advertising campaign saw Rosebud Dolls Ltd promote two new dolls – 'Wonder Baby' and the 'Chatty Cathy Talking Doll'. The manufacturers boasted that 'no celebrity had ever been accorded as much press and television coverage', including three months of ITV adverts and coverage in all the mass circulation women's magazines.

Pedigree's iconic doll, Sindy, arrived in 1963 to rival the USA's Barbie, alongside Action Man, the first doll specifically targeted at boys. Sindy became the year's best seller, even starring in her own TV commercial wearing Mary Quant dresses. Advertised as a 'free, swinging, grown-up girl', she was very different from 1950s baby dolls. Initially there were plans to give Sindy a boyfriend, Paul, after Paul McCartney from the Beatles, but the idea was never adopted. Traditional dolls and dolls' houses, prams and push chairs remained popular but the new-style dolls were more like real babies, such as Palitoy's Tiny Tears. Tricycles and bicycles were still common, but when Raleigh Chopper bicycles 'with gears' arrived in 1969, they became the 'cool' bike of the decade.

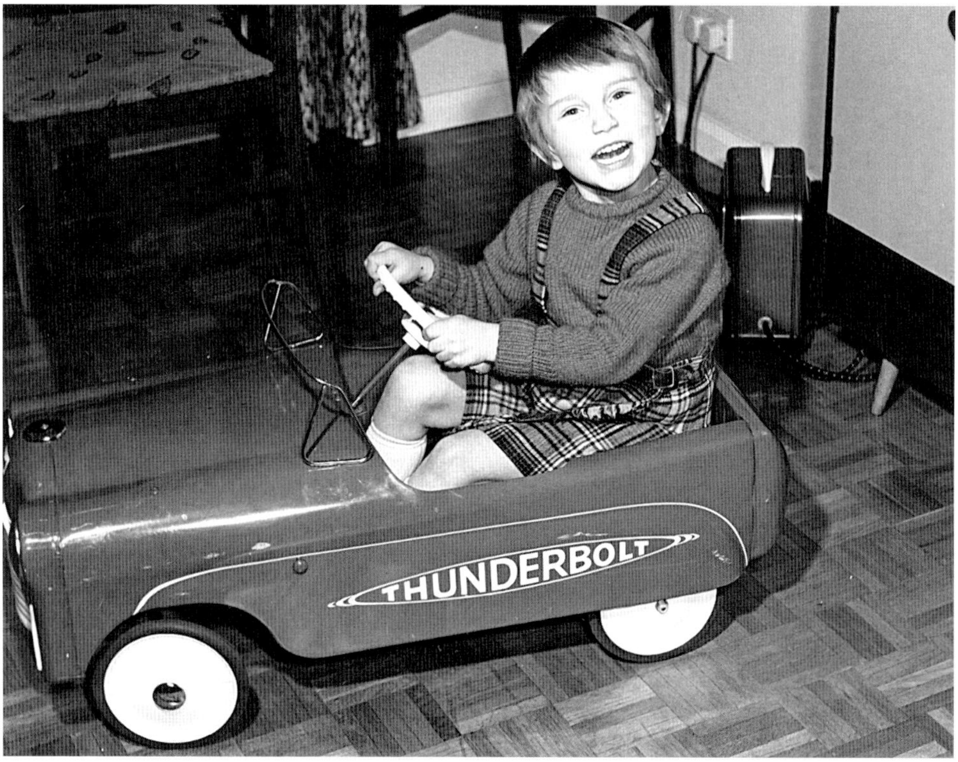

Sally Martin riding in her Thunderbolt toy pedal car. Toys were generally gender-based across the 1960s and most advertisements for toy cars were targeted at boys. (Sally Jones)

Did you know?

In 1962, Nottingham bicycle firm Raleigh supplied seven bicycles from their Sunbeam range for use in a touring production of *Snow White and the Seven Dwarfs*. In Southsea, Liverpool, Nottingham, Bradford and Newcastle, Sunbeam dealers staged special window displays to advertise both their bikes and the Dwarfs' tour. British Toys, 1962.

The famous interlocking plastic toy bricks made by Danish company Lego took the UK by storm in the early 1960s. By 1964, the firm were producing whole sets with step by step building instructions. Lego became one of the most successful toys, not only of the decade, but the twentieth century. Other sought-after toys in the sixties included Scalextric, Dinky cars, Etch a Sketch, Sindy, Action Man and 'Spacehoppers'. Spirograph arrived – an educational drawing toy designed by a British electronic engineer, Denys Fisher, who was working on bomb designs for NATO. Toys from television's *Magic Roundabout* grew in popularity. Although sales had declined since the mid-fifties, Meccano was still popular. In 1965, the National Association of Toy Retailers introduced Toy of the Year Awards. The first went to Corgi's famous James Bond Aston Martin car, one of Mark's most prized possessions, 'as featured in *Goldfinger*, with the little ejector seat'. Subsequent awards went to Action Man, Spirograph, Sindy and, in 1969, Hot Wheels cars.

Remembering his 1960s childhood, Stephen Wade recalled: 'I painted model soldiers most days after school and had a range of toy guns hung on a pegboard that fired caps, available in many stores at a penny a roll.' He also had Lego and Betta Builda and played board games with the family, such as Monopoly, Formula 1, Mousetrap and Cluedo. His favourite game was Diplomacy, 'which could take two days to complete ... the king of strategic games'. Across the decade, developments in Britain's toy industry reflected the modern 'spirit of the times'. The country's economic expansion and the exciting progress of science and technology brought immeasurable changes to the recreational life of most British children.

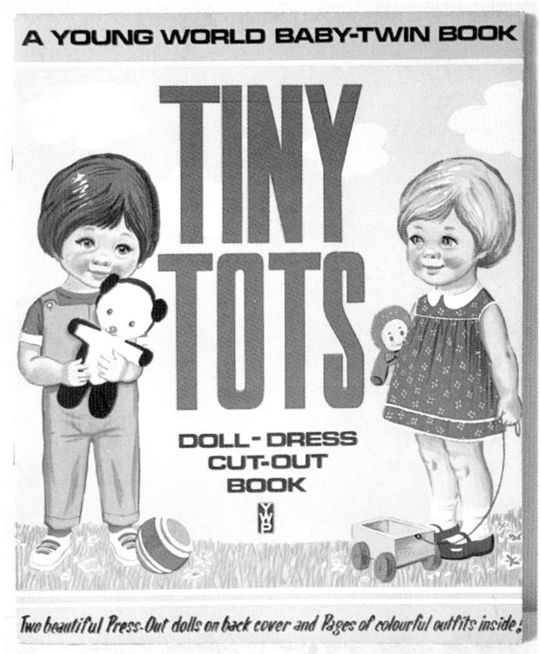

Dressing cardboard cut-out dolls was a very popular pastime for young girls. The clothes had flaps to hook them onto the dolls.

1960s toys marketed for girls: a doll with a modern short hairstyle and a fold-up dolls' pushchair with folding rain cover and hood. (Karen Livingstone)

Royal Mail Christmas stamps were first issued in 1966 with a set of children's paintings chosen following a *Blue Peter* competition. Two years later in 1968, a set of stamps featured children's toys. (Stamp designs © Royal Mail Group Ltd)

7
What Now?

For those readers wanting to pursue an interest in the history of childhood, there are societies that provide a useful starting point, such as:

Society for the Study of Childhood in the Past
https://sscip.wordpress.com
Department of Archaeology, Durham University, South Road, Durham, DH1 3LE
This is an interdisciplinary society that promotes all aspects of the study of childhood in the past.

Centre for the History of Childhood
https://www.history.ox.ac.uk
University of Oxford, Faculty of History, George Street, Oxford OX1 2RL
Researches the history of childhood and encourages links between historians and childcare professionals.

History of Education Society
historyofeducation.org.uk
History of Education Society, University of Glasgow, St Andrews Building, 11, Eldon Street, Glasgow G3 6NH
Promotes the study and teaching of the history of education and provides opportunities for discussion.

Further Reading

Brewer, Susan, *British Dolls of the 1960s* (Pen and Sword, 2009).
Explains which 1960s dolls are worth collecting, and the new sixties style dolls aimed at teenagers.
Hill, Tim et al, *The Beatles: The Illustrated Biography* (Transatlantic Press, 2008).
The story of the Beatles, the group that defined pop music in the sixties.
Johnson, Alan, *This Boy: A Memoir of Childhood* (Bantam Press, 2013).
In this award-winning biography, Alan Johnson, MP and former Home Secretary, describes growing up in 1960s London in poverty, condemned housing and poor health.
Jones, Christine, *A Northampton Childhood in the 1960s* (Amberley, 2014).
Based on recollections of a 1960s Midlands childhood, recounting time spent at school, at home and at public events.
Macpherson, Gordon, *Our NHS: A Celebration of 50 Years* (BMJ Books, 1998).
A history of the Britain's National Health Service to commemorate the fiftieth anniversary of the NHS, written by distinguished figures in medicine and politics.
Press Association Ltd, *The 1960s: Britain in Pictures* (A&E Publications, 2008).

Contains around 300 photographs from the 1960s 'that helped shape the people and face of Britain'.
Sandbrook, Dominic, *White Heat: A History of Britain in the Swinging Sixties* (Abacus, 2009).
A readable and substantial contribution to the history of Britain in the 1960s.
Tait, Derek, *1960s Childhood: Moon Landings, The Kinks and the 1966 World Cup* (Amberley, 2014).
Tait describes growing up in a decade of 'innovation, fashion, television and music'.
Woodcock, Joan, *Matron Knows Best* (Headline Publishing Group, 2012).
Joan Woodcock's life in nursing from a sixteen-year-old cadet in 1966 to working on hospital wards, casualty units and in the community.
Yurdan, Marilyn, *School Songs and Gym Slips: Grammar Schools in the 1950s and 1960s* (The History Press, 2012).
With a foreword by Theresa May MP, Yurdan provides memories and details that will resound with thousands of ex-grammar school girls.

Places to visit

The Willis Museum, Market Place, Basingstoke RG21 7QD
Tel: 01256 366283
www.hampshireculturaltrust.org.uk
The museum has a 1960s kitchen full of contemporary items. A photograph of the Willis kitchen is included in this book.

The Museum Of Brands, Packaging and Advertising, 111–117, Lancaster Road, Notting Hill W111QT
Tel: 0207 243 9611
www.museumofbrands.com
Robert Opie's museum examines the history of consumer culture from Victorian times to the present day, including numerous household items from the 1960s.

Victoria and Albert Museum, Cromwell Road, Knightsbridge, London SW7 2RL
Tel: 0207 942 2000
www.vam.ac.uk
The V&A holds a collection of 1960s fashion including the iconic miniskirt and the revolution in youthful fashions.

Museum of Childhood, Cambridge Heath Road, London E2 9PA
Tel: 0208 983 5200
www.vam.ac.uk/moc
The museum displays toys, dolls, games and childhood exhibits from across the decades with exhibitions and activities for all ages.

York Castle Museum, Eye of York, York YO1 9RY
Tel: 01904 687687
www.yorkcastlemuseum.org.uk

The Sixties gallery recreates the period, with objects such as a Lambretta scooter, a Dansette record player, Beatles singles and Mary Quant fashions.

Whitby Museum, Pannett Park, Whitby YO21 1RE
Tel: 01947 602908
https://whitbymuseum.org.uk
The museum has a large, varied and ever growing collection of toys, dolls, books and games.

Roald Dahl Museum and Story Telling Centre, 81–83, High Street, Great Missenden, Bucks HP16 0AL
Tel: 01494 892192
www.roalddahl.com>museum
The museum houses all Dahl's main papers and his 'Ideas Books'. It holds regular workshops and events for creative writing. In 2008, the museum won Enjoy England's 'Best Small Visitor Attraction' award.

The Fashion Museum, Assembly Rooms, Bennett Street, Bath BA1 2QH
Tel: 01225 477789
www.fashionmuseum.co.uk
The museum opened in 1963 with Langley Moore's fashion collection and focusses on fashionable clothes from the late sixteenth century to the present day, with more than 100,000 exhibits.

Pollock's Toy Museum, 1 Scala Street, Bloomsbury, London W1T 2HL
Tel: 0207 636 3452
www.pollockstoys.com
A feast for toy lovers, designed and created in the 1950s and 1960s. The exhibits are mainly Victorian but with some twentieth-century toys.

Museum of Liverpool, Pier Head, Liverpool Waterfront, Liverpool, L3 1DG
Tel: 0151 478 4545
www.liverpoolmuseums.org
Exhibits include fashion, school, leisure, shopping and music from the 1960s.

Websites

General information, images and 1960s items can be sourced at **www.amazon.co.uk** and on the image-collecting site **Pinterest** (specifically https://uk.pinterest.com/1960sdecor).
The film *The Boat That Rocked*, set in 1966, based on the pirate radio stations between 1964 and 1967, is on DVD, 2009. Genre: Comedy. Director: Richard Curtis. Rating: 15. EAN: 5050582702309.

The Way We Were – A 1960s Childhood by SpringChicken
https://springchicken.co.uk>then-and-now (16 October 2017)
The website recalls the sixties, e.g. Ladybird's Peter and Jane books, indoor bathrooms, BBC Radio's *Music, Mime and Movement*, corporal punishment, transistor radios, TV favourites, etc.

Learn About the 'Swinging' Sixties
www.retrowow.co.uk/60s.html
Memories from the sixties include fashion, TV, interior design, cars, Mods, Rockers, Hippies, the Beatles, Rolling Stones, etc.

History of the BBC in the 1960s
www.bbc.co.uk>timelines
Describes the growth of colour television. Focusses on some famous BBC TV dramas like *Doctor Who* from 1963 and *The Forsyte Saga* (1967).

The 1960s: The Decade that Shook Britain by Kimberley Watson
www.historic-uk.com>CultureUK
A short, impressive essay by seventeen-year-old Kimberley describes the 'swinging' sixties.

25 photographs that show the brutal reality of poverty in 1960s /1970s Manchester...
https://www.manchestereveningnews.com
Disturbing photographs of child poverty in the 1960s in Manchester and Salford, photographed over four years by Nick Hedges for the charity Shelter. In 2016, a quest was launched to trace the children in the pictures.

Your 1960s: Life At Home – BBC News Magazine
www.news.bbc.co.uk/2/hi/uk_news.bbc.co.uk/6707451.stm
Written contributions, photographs and memories of home life from the generation who grew up in 1960s Britain.

Making a new life in 1960s Britain. Operation Black Vote – The Home of Black Politics
www.obv.org.uk>News
Operation Black Vote (OBV) intern Natalie Simmons writes about her grandmother's life in 1960s Britain after arriving from the Caribbean island of Grenada.

SAGA – Ten iconic moments that capture 1960s Britain
https://www.saga.co.uk>nostalgia>Ten-iconic-moments-of-the-1960s
Photographs and text covering important landmarks in 1960s Britain, including politics, pop music, pirate radio, transport and sport, as well as Charles's investiture as Prince of Wales.

V&A An Introduction to 1960s. Fashion.
https://www.vam.ac.uk>articles>an-introductionto
The website focusses on innovative designers from the sixties and the 1960s market for youth fashion.

Life in 60s Britain; British Life in the 1960s; Mid-1960s Suburban Life in the UK
https://m.youtube.com
Three-and-a-half-minute Chaz Mork film about life in 1960s Britain (2013).
Twenty-four-minute Huntley Film Archives film of British life in the 1960s: film 30707 (2012).
Fifty-seven-second clips and footage film – Mid-1960s Suburban Life in the UK (2013).